THE NATURE OF WHAT'S TO COME™

A Century of Innovation

1902   1912   1922   1932   1942   1952   1962   1972   1982   1992   2002

The Nature of What's to Come™

A Century of Innovation

Archer Daniels Midland Company

1902-2002

A Century of Innovation

Publisher's Cataloging-in-Publication Data
    The nature of what's to come : a century of Innovation.
    – Decatur, Ill.: Archer Daniels Midland, 2002.
        p. ; cm.

ISBN 0-9724614-0-X
    1. Archer Daniels Midland Company. 2. Farm corporations –
    History. 3. Farm Corporations – Forecasting. I. Archer Daniels
    Midland Company.

HD2731 .N38 2002   2002112520
338.1 - - dc21   0301

60 05 04 03 02 * 5 4 3 2 1

Project Coordination by Jenkins Group Inc. * www.bookpublishing.com
Design by Jennifer Allen

Printed in the United States of America

This book is dedicated to the past and present employees of Archer Daniels Midland Company.

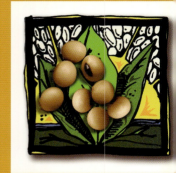

OILSEED PROCESSING, FOOD INGREDIENTS, ETHANOL, BIOFUELS AND INDUSTRIALS, NATURAL HEALTH AND NUTRITION, FEED INGREDIENTS, COCOA, GRAIN, TRANSPORTATION

Contents

The world has changed in many ways over the course of ADM's 100 year history. Advances in technology have transformed the way we all live, work and communicate. In agriculture alone, the past century has seen farming go from the horse-powered past to the modern, high-tech present. We enter the next century with newly discovered knowledge regarding genetics and a newly founded understanding of the role foods and diet play in human health that places us on the cusp of a second agricultural revolution.

As agriculture has changed, so too has ADM. Today, what was once proudly described as the leading flaxseed processor in southern Minnesota has grown to be the leading food processor in the world. We produce a vastly expanded supply of numerous food, animal feed and renewable fuel products that meet the pressing needs of an ever-growing world. And increasingly, we are using cutting-edge technology to unlock the hidden value of our raw material stream by developing new, naturally based products that fit into unique niches and provide answers to vexing problems.

The one constant that has not changed in our Company history is the critical value of our people. ADM employees, from John W. Daniels in 1902 down to the most recent hire, are the heart and soul of this Company. Their dedication allows ADM to remain focused, drives our creativity and enables constant innovation.

This book is a window into the hard work of the last hundred years- of the accomplishments, the culture and occasions that together have shaped Archer Daniels Midland Company. Together with all of our past and present employees, I am proud to have played a part.

G. Allen Andreas
Chairman and Chief Executive

While I have been part of the ADM family for only ten of the Company's 100 years, my admiration of our Company dates back to the very start of my career in 1972. I was working as a grain merchandiser for another agribusiness concern. Attending my first industry trade show, I was very impressed by the enthusiasm that the people from ADM exhibited when they talked about their jobs and their company. "I need to work with people like that … at a company like that," was my first thought. It only took me a little while to find out that there was only one "company like that" – Archer Daniels Midland Company.

ADM offers a unique and rewarding atmosphere to all of its employees. Indeed, I believe that what makes ADM a special company is its employees. It may be a little like the chicken-and-egg question. It's hard to know which came first; an outstanding group of dedicated people who created an entrepreneurial and rewarding corporate culture; or a unique culture that helps to develop outstanding employees. I like to think that our people and our culture work together to strengthen each other and the Company as a whole.

In the course of our 100 years, ADM has grown from a small regional oilseed processor to a global agribusiness powerhouse, providing the world with high quality food ingredients, feed ingredients and renewable fuels. There are very few companies who have played such an instrumental role in the economy and lives of so many people spread across the globe.

As the Company has expanded and evolved, one thing has remained constant: the ADM spirit to innovate and to achieve. This book is a testament to that spirit and to the thousands of people who have played a part, both large and small, in our 100-year long story of success.

Paul B. Mulhollem
President and COO

THE NATURE OF WHAT'S TO COME

The Nature of What's to Come™

A Century of Innovation

Archer Daniels Midland Company

ADM HISTORY

1902–2002

ADM Picnic – July 4, 1950

THE NATURE OF WHAT'S TO COME™: A CENTURY OF INNOVATION

The Nature of What's to Come: A Century of Innovation is a celebration of the culture and entrepreneurial spirit that make ADM unique. Determination, ingenuity and ability have made our first one hundred years a century of achievement.

For decades, the world has looked to ADM for products and ideas that improve standards of living and eliminate hunger and malnutrition. These challenges have always been central to our calling. Our corporate mission – to unlock the potential of nature to improve the quality of life – is not only the foundation of our proud past, it is truly "The Nature of What's to Come."

It's been said that the past is prologue. If that's true, and we believe it is, the twenty-first century holds untold promise for ADM. We are as diversified as the world we serve, and our products are essential to the basic needs of all humanity. We aggressively invest in innovation and growth. We are firmly resolved to deliver maximum value to our shareholders. We are socially and environmentally responsible. We are committed to making the world a better place – for our shareholders, for our customers, for our employees and for the world at large.

But there is one factor that stands above the rest. Everything at ADM begins with our employees – the source of innovation, of process improvements and of the hard work and dedication that translate into finished products and enduring success – the soul of ADM.

Much of our culture can be understood by the remarks made by John H. Daniels, former ADM chairman, nearly fifty years ago: "In a free enterprise system such as we enjoy in this nation, profit is the reward for ability and effort. In large measure, the survival of our system will depend on the continuing ability and determination of industry to provide gainful employment and an ever-increasing standard of living at home and abroad. ADM is building to meet these challenges in its special field of endeavor – the processing of agricultural and food products."

It is this ability and determination that will continue to make ADM a leader in the twenty-first century.

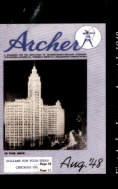

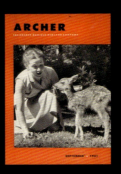

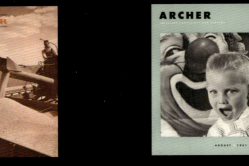

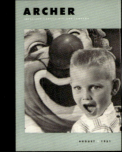

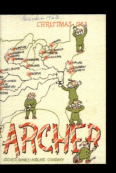

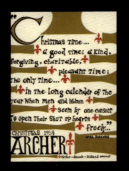

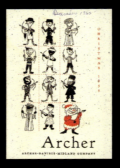

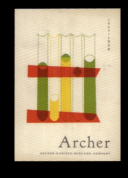

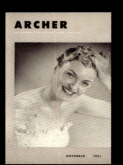

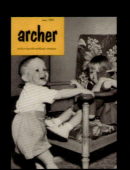

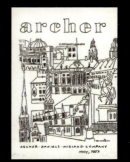

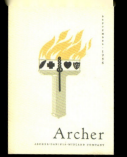

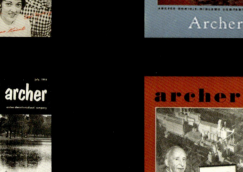

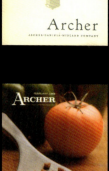

ARCHER • DANIELS

George A. Archer

John W. Daniels

A QUICK GLANCE

Through ADM's first decade, founders John W. Daniels and George A. Archer worked from an office in a one-story building adjoining their mill in Minneapolis, where workers ground flaxseed to make linseed oil. They addressed each other as "Mr. Archer" and "Mr. Daniels" and sat facing each other at roll-top desks, closely supervising every detail of their growing operation. Lunch was a sandwich and sometimes soup, stewed on the spot. A young bookkeeper, Samuel Mairs, who would become chairman years later, shared the office with them. The office was noisy, full of the clatter of machinery and permeated with the aroma of linseed oil.

Over the next one hundred years, the brainchild of Mr. Archer and Mr. Daniels grew to be about far more than flax and linseed oil. We've come far from our humble beginnings, but to understand ADM today, we must look first at what gave rise to ADM.

Transportation in our early years was limited, and all of our customers were within the United States.

A FOUNDATION OF FLAX

Ever since prehistoric times, flax has been one of mankind's most useful plants. In the Stone Age, people gathered flaxseed for food and flax stems for the fibers from which they made ropes and fishnets and cloth. Ancient Egyptians used flax to weave fine linens, including those for mummy wrappings. While it is not currently used so, the seed of the flax plant, called linseed, was an important source of food in Greek and Roman times. The drying properties of linseed oil were probably recognized very early, and it was used widely throughout the ancient world as a drying oil.

Until the invention of the cotton gin in 1793, flax was the most important vegetable fiber in the world, cultivated extensively throughout Europe until the end of the eighteenth century.

Because early settlers who came to this continent brought the seeds that would furnish them linen, the flax crop is closely identified with the settlement of the United States. Along with the westward movement of the frontier moved flax, not only a useful crop but one that yielded a particularly bountiful harvest on newly broken sod.

But farmers with flax weren't the only pioneers heading west. In 1902, John W. Daniels, encouraged by George A. Archer, came to Minneapolis to found the Daniels Linseed Company. The following year, Archer joined Daniels, and in 1905 the Company name was changed to the Archer Daniels Linseed Company. The two men, friends since the time when both were in the linseed oil business in Ohio's Miami Valley, were well qualified for their venture. The Archer family had been crushing flaxseed since the 1830's, and Daniels had entered the flax crushing business in 1879.

The "Golden Age of Agriculture"

According to ADM's "Articles of Incorporation," the new Company commenced business on September 30, 1902, for the purpose of "manufacturing flax and other seeds and cereals into their natural products and to sell the products so manufactured by it." As was so often the case throughout the twentieth century, ADM's timing and entrepreneurial instincts couldn't have been better.

While the industrial revolution had rapidly changed the face of everyday life in America, agriculture had also undergone a revolution no less momentous, which included a shift from hand labor to machine farming and from subsistence farming to commercial agriculture. As a result, from the period following the Civil War to 1910, the number of farms tripled – increasing from two million to six million – while the amount of land being cultivated more than doubled from 395 million to 870 million acres.

In ADM, American farmers got an invaluable resource and partner as ADM helped them find new uses, markets and distribution methods for their produce. During this period the average gross income of farms more than doubled and the value of those farms more than tripled.

At the same time, by reinvesting most of its earnings back into the Company, ADM grew rapidly. During the first ten years, production capacity tripled and capitalization increased almost eight times, reaching $1,000,000 in 1911. Remarkably, in an example of strength and fortitude that would be essential for ADM throughout the twentieth century, the Company achieved this growth despite two economic depressions, one in 1903 and another in 1907.

At the advent of World War I, the U.S. cut its duty on flaxseed and began to encourage imports. As a result, eastern mills, which could import seed from abroad, crush it and sell it more cheaply than western mills, gained an important advantage.

Fortunately, ADM's founders displayed the hallmarks of a culture that would serve well over the ensuing decades by rapidly responding to their new environment with ingenuity and determination. In order to compete in the eastern market, the Company built a linseed mill and a one and a half million bushel public grain elevator at Buffalo, New York, in 1915. However, this wasn't the firm's first venture outside of Minneapolis. In 1914, a mill had been leased at Superior, Wisconsin, and the Toledo Seed and Oil Company, which crushed flaxseed and castor beans, was acquired in 1917.

The first Company ledger included entries from October 17, 1902 – April 13, 1904.

October 30, 1929 — All of the early presidents and chairmen of Archer Daniels Midland Company. This photograph includes both Mr. J.W. Daniels and Mr. G. A. Archer, the two founders of ADM and their spouses. It also includes the sons of the founders: Shreve M. Archer and Thomas L. Daniels, who both became presidents of ADM and their spouses. In addition, Samuel Mairs, who served as chairman of ADM and his wife are also pictured. All of the other guests at the party were close friends of Mr. and Mrs. J.W. Daniels.

THE 1920'S — A TIME FOR GROWTH

With the advent of the 1920's, increased U.S. demand for flaxseed encouraged a burgeoning import market for the commodity. In order to lower transportation costs and establish a processing facility close to the east coast ports into which flax was shipped, the Company built a linseed crushing plant at Edgewater, New Jersey, in 1922. The capacity at Minneapolis was also expanded in 1922 by leasing the Northern Linseed Company Mill.

The year 1923 marked the formation of the present Archer Daniels Midland Company. The Midland Linseed Products Company was, like Archer-Daniels, one of the leading firms in the industry. Originally incorporated in 1902, Midland Linseed Products Company was very successful. Over the years, operations were expanded to include mills at Chicago, Toledo and Edgewater, New Jersey. With the merger, its plants at Minneapolis and Edgewater adjoined those of Archer-Daniels and the new Company became the world's largest producer of linseed oil. Its nine mills contained a total of 334 presses, one out of every three in the country. ADM had made an important decision — to shift the firm from a small business to a leader in its field.

Under the guidance of Shreve M. Archer, who had succeeded John W. Daniels as president in 1924, ADM began a long and extensive program of continued growth and diversification. The Company was already the largest crusher of flaxseed, but Shreve M. Archer made it still larger through purchases that during his first four years as president increased ADM's capacity by fifty percent, giving it a total of 518 presses.

Most of the expansion took place in 1928. The William O. Goodrich Company of Milwaukee had been in the flaxseed business since 1875, and although it did not rank as one of the largest crushers, it had thirty presses and did an excellent business in special and refined linseed oils, making it an attractive purchase for ADM.

The Fredonia Linseed Oil Works had been built in 1892 when Fredonia, Kansas, was the center of an important flax producing area. ADM took over the twelve-press mill on July 1, 1928.

For many years the lion's share of flaxseed crushing had been handled by four firms, and then, after the merger of Archer-Daniels and Midland, by three: ADM, Spencer Kellogg and Sons and the American Linseed Oil Company. By a contract signed July 20, 1928, ADM and Spencer Kellogg agreed to a joint purchase of American's linseed operations. With the deal, ADM got the twelve-press Portland Linseed Company of Portland, Oregon, a barreling station in East Cambridge, Massachusetts, and the Dean Mill on Staten Island that had been the largest in the world when it was built near the turn of the century.

After these purchases there remained no new worlds to conquer, at least in the linseed world. ADM and Spencer Kellogg stood head and shoulders above the industry.

Already there were indications that Shreve M. Archer had his eyes set on other horizons. In 1925, ADM had built the concrete grain elevator called Delmar No. 3. Though it had been operating the Dellwood Elevator in Buffalo for eight years, this was ADM's first elevator property in Minneapolis. In 1927, when the Armour Grain Company of Chicago was forced into liquidation and had to dispose of its Great Northern and Delmar Elevators in Minneapolis, ADM bought them, adding two more elevators with a capacity of two million bushels. With this purchase, ADM's grain division was formed to handle elevator operations, and the policy of diversification, moving ADM beyond the crushing of flaxseed, was launched.

ADM took two more significant steps toward diversifying its activities in 1929. Converting the Toledo and Chicago plants to the crushing of soybeans did not seem momentous at the time, since the United States was just becoming aware of the potential value of the soybean. Though soybeans were a relatively new crop in the United States, their economic importance and value would grow substantially in the coming decades. Not even the coming Depression could hold back the soybean industry that made its greatest strides when economic conditions were at their worst. Farmers, seeing that soybeans were a profitable crop, boosted production more than threefold to produce forty-nine million bushels in 1935, and nearly doubled that figure with the ninety million bushel harvest of 1939.

This tremendous increase in the crop reflected a corresponding increase in the demand for soybean products. Soybean oil could be used in margarine, shortening and salad oil. Soybean oil meal could be used in livestock and poultry feeds and could also be made into soy flour, an important ingredient in candy, baked goods, prepared mixes, macaroni products and high protein bread. Also, the soybean became an important ingredient in a host of industrial products as varied as plastics, cosmetics, wallboard, paper coatings, insecticides, paint, ethyl gasoline and plywood.

At the time, the purchase on October 9, 1929, of the Werner G. Smith Company of Cleveland, Ohio, a manufacturer of core oils and an importer and processor of foreign and marine oils, seemed far more important. This company was the largest producer of core oils, a category of base synthetic oils that can be interchanged among each other for various industrial purposes. The principal ingredient of core oils, linseed oil, it purchased in quantity from ADM. By acquiring this company, ADM was able to sell a considerable quantity of its oil as a finished product, commanding a better profit than raw linseed oil.

Although ADM was just beginning to feel the developing Depression, some companies had already been having a difficult time. The Commander-Larabee Corporation, then ranking as one of the largest milling companies, was in a financial condition that made further bank credit impossible. ADM came to the rescue, advancing money to Commander and assuming its management. This agreement led to the eventual acquisition of Commander-Larabee by ADM.

By 1930, the groundwork had been laid for the future development of ADM. Though flaxseed crushing still remained the chief business, it was by this time only one of many diversified operations.

The new phase of development that ADM was entering would not be witnessed by the two men who had watched over the Company from the days when it had a net worth of $125,000 and one mill. Under their guidance it had become a $15,500,000 corporation whose properties spanned the continent and whose business involved worldwide operations. The two men so closely associated for such a long period died in successive years, John W. Daniels on June 8, 1931, at the age of seventy-four, and George A. Archer on November 12, 1932, at the age of eighty-two.

Circa 1950

Key

Administration Office
Sales Offices
Linseed & Soybean Mills
Flour Mills
Feed Mills
Grain Terminal Elevators
Fish Oil Plants
Laboratories
Flax Fibre Mills
Varnish Plants
Country Elevators

ALOHA! Gooch's '77 BEST FEEDS

Red Wing, Minnesota Plant
Photograph courtesy of Phil Revoir Historical Collection.

THE 1930's – A DECADE OF CONTRASTS

Despite the profound economic and societal devastation wrought by the Great Depression, ADM was able to achieve much in the 1930's. Instead of waiting for conditions to improve, ADM proactively pushed ahead, developing new products, entering new markets and ramping up research. This policy, which brought immediate returns as well as long-range benefits, enabled ADM to turn the Depression years into a productive period.

An extraordinary number of projects were introduced at that time. Between 1930 and 1932, the storage capacity of the grain division increased by eleven million bushels. In 1931, ADM began merchandising formula feeds, a combination of specific ingredients mixed to meet the nutritional needs of various types of livestock. It began manufacturing these feeds in 1933. It installed the first continuous solvent extraction unit in the U.S. at the Chicago plant in 1934 and began the solvent extraction of soybeans. The Company's research laboratory dates from 1934, and the first chemical processing operations started the following year. The flax fiber plant was acquired in 1939 and that same year ADM began modernizing its linseed mills by converting to expeller presses. During the Depression, ADM expanded operations on both the east and west coasts and established a Canadian subsidiary, Archer Daniels Midland Company (Canada) Ltd.

Historically, the low point of the Depression occurred in 1932, but by then the tide had already started to turn at ADM. Despite falling sales, earnings were on the upswing and in 1935, ADM achieved a record net profit of $2,500,000 dollars on $57,000,000 in net sales. To mark the milestone, ADM declared a special dividend of one dollar in addition to the annual one-dollar distribution.

As late as 1932, ADM's entire technical staff consisted of five people, but when a new laboratory was completed the following year, staff grew. By 1935, the research and product control staff numbered eighteen. At that time, the ADM laboratory was the most modern and best equipped of its kind in the country. Not only did the chemists conduct regular tests to ensure uniform product quality, they also worked constantly toward new and improved products for the industry.

Through aggressive research, ADM developed the solvent extraction process for removing oil from the soybean and for applying the same process to linseed oil. The research staff's efforts were aimed at using heat to create new soybean oil products, new paint formulations, new core oils for foundry molds and finer baking flours. It was ADM's research staff that later turned previously useless flax straw into materials that would be used for fine writing paper, cigarette papers and U.S. currency. These discoveries alone added millions to the income of U.S. farmers.

By the end of the decade, grain storage at ADM had expanded considerably, beyond Minneapolis to other parts of the country. This expansion included the addition of sixteen million bushels of capacity, all leased and acquired through the purchase of branch offices in Omaha, Nebraska; Duluth, Minnesota; and Portland, Oregon. This brought ADM two mammoth elevators — a three-million-bushel elevator at Vancouver, Washington, which was the largest on the west coast, and an eleven-million-bushel elevator at Superior, Wisconsin, one of the world's largest.

THE 1940'S — THE TRANSFORMATION FROM AGRICULTURE TO INDUSTRY

By the early 1940's, America's transformation from an agricultural and rural society to an industrial and urban society was well under way. While the nation's population increased and there were ever more mouths to feed, modern farming methods and sophisticated machinery enabled farmers to cultivate larger areas and produce more crops with greater efficiency. Though the long and tortuous decade of the 1930s had threatened America's way of life, the story of American agriculture was one of triumph instead of defeat.

And as the nation's farmers fought to help America recover from the Depression, another battle – World War II – threatened millions all over the globe and required the maximum effort of every citizen.

When World War II broke out, ADM prepared for and helped to meet the nation's tremendous need for oils, fats, flours, foundry products and chemicals, receiving citations from the U.S. government for its production accomplishments during the emergency years.

ADM research chemists redoubled their efforts to improve products and create advanced materials. New product development began to grow rapidly, so that an increasingly large share of ADM's output oil was sold in refined or chemically processed form. Raw linseed oil and crude soybean oil were turned into several hundred different products. Since these required special selling techniques and a thorough understanding of their uses and applications, the research laboratory supplied chemists, known as technical sales servicemen, who assisted both the sales department and ADM customers.

The research program was expanded in 1943 when it was recognized that improving ADM products, working out new applications for them and above all, developing new products, was to be a major factor in Company growth. Though the research department had outgrown its quarters, it was impossible to put up a new building during the war. Fortunately, ADM was able to lease the former Johnson School in Minneapolis to which the research department and its staff of sixty moved in July of 1945. Within three years, the accelerated research efforts made possible by the move developed twenty-four new products in the field of drying oils alone. Besides working on the development of new products, on production research and on sales service, the general research laboratory acted as a consultant to all the divisions of ADM.

At ADM, research had won an important place for itself because it had proved its worth on the books of the Company. Time and again lagging sales of raw and semi-processed products were offset by gains in new products and specialties. The four-fold increase in net sales between 1939 and 1949 was attributed largely to new products and new methods developed through research.

New construction was out of the question during World War II, but ADM was constantly looking ahead, appraising its facilities and planning for the future. Within a few months after the war ended, the Company started building a new mill at Mankato, Minnesota, for the feed division. When the mill started operating in 1946, it provided a much-needed addition to ADM's feed mixing capacity. Although commercial mixed feeds had been available since the beginning of the century and had come into wide acceptance during the 1920's, the feed industry did not become really important until it suddenly mushroomed during World War II.

In 1939, the U.S. had used thirteen million tons of prepared animal feed, but by 1943 this had risen to twenty-nine million tons. To increase the production of livestock and poultry during the war, federal and state agricultural education programs stressed the value of mixed feeds to supply the protein necessary for efficient production of livestock. Although the protein concentrates used in formula feeds included oil meal made from flaxseed, soybeans, cottonseed, peanuts and copra and also included mill feeds, milk products and meat scraps, the growing demand for protein concentrates was filled largely by soybean oil meal. Soybean oil meal showed a four-million-ton increase in production between 1939 and 1954 while protein concentrates in general showed less than half that much gain.

As one of the largest processors of soybean oil meal, ADM helped to fill the increasing demand for formula feed by meeting the needs of a large portion of the industry as well as filling the requirements of its own expanding feed division. ADM bought the Dickinson feed plant in 1945 and operated it until 1953 when it was closed because of high production costs. In the meantime, the Mankato mill, equipped for continuous-flow processing, was considerably enlarged. In addition, a molasses feed plant was set up at the Winona flax fiber plant, where parts of the shive (a short woody core fiber produced by flax) were ground as a base for beef and dairy feeds.

Commander-Larabee had also built up an active feed department, which produced livestock and poultry feeds at Marysville and Wellington, Kansas – former flour mills converted to manufacturing commercial feed. Twenty-two of the Commander-Larabee elevators also served as local feed mixing plants.

ADM emerged from the war with broad plans for growth in many areas. Between 1945 and 1947, the Company leased an oil mill at Ganado, Texas, purchased the Twin City "A" Elevator at Minneapolis, Minnesota, and began expansion of its west coast grain operations, as well as grain elevator facilities throughout Minnesota. ADM's net assets in 1946 were fifty million dollars – more than five times what they had been when the Company was incorporated in 1923. Working capital exceeded twenty-nine million dollars, compared with less than four million dollars twenty-three years earlier.

In 1947, following the death of Shreve M. Archer, who had fostered the growth and expansion of ADM for twenty-three years as president, Thomas L. Daniels became president of ADM. As a young man, Mr. Daniels had joined the Company his father founded before leaving to serve in the U.S. Diplomatic Corps. He returned to ADM in 1929, but during World War II had been called to government service as chief of the Fats and Oils Branch of the War Food Administration. He rejoined ADM in 1946 as executive vice president and became president the following year. Samuel Mairs, the one-time bookkeeper and assistant to the Company's founders, was elected chairman of the board.

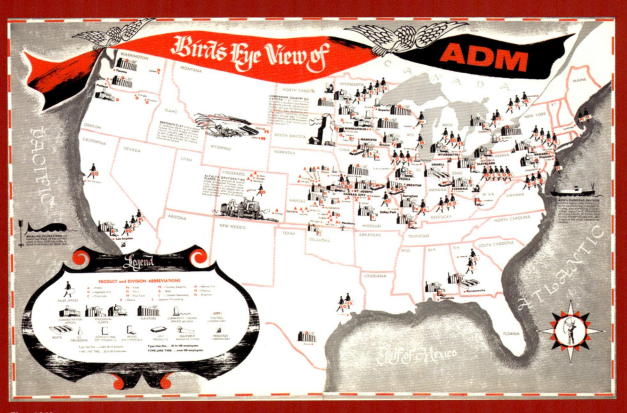

Circa 1960

November 11, 1952

50 Years of Progress

We've just celebrated an important birthday. It was just 50 years ago that John W. Daniels established the Company which was destined to become one of the world's leading processors of agricultural crops.

Looking back at the philosophy of its founders, we can see some of the reasons why, despite its humble beginnings, the young firm was destined to attain its present leadership in the industry.

John Daniels and George Archer believed in production. "Year around production at low margins," was their creed. This is the very principle which has, perhaps more than anything else, helped make America the great industrial power it is today.

There's another reason why our Company has steadily forged ahead. Here, again, we must pay tribute to the foresight of the founders for it was their determination to make a better product which caused them to turn to science as an ally.

Today, the little Company, which began with its single linseed mill back in 1902, operates 120 plants scattered from coast to coast. No longer entirely dependent upon the manufacture of linseed oil, it now consists of twelve major divisions: flaxseed, soybean, flour, chemical products, foundry products, livestock and poultry feeds, alfalfa meal, grain, chlorophyll, fibre, industrial cereals, and Archer-Daniels-Midland Limited, our Canadian subsidiary.

And research is playing a more vital part at ADM than ever before. New products, new applications, and new markets are being created in our laboratories. Whether it's linseed oil or cake flour, flax fibre or chlorophyll, we're continually discovering new ways to improve upon nature.

As we enter our second 50 years, the twin principles of maximum production and continual product improvement still guide your Company. Just as we've pioneered for the past half century, we shall continue to pioneer. And today's horizons are brighter than ever.

T. L. Daniels, President

50 Years of Progress

ADM President, T.L. Daniels and Sam Mairs inspect the machinery at a Special Oils Plant. Sam Mairs started with the Company when he was twenty years old. He was both a bookkeeper and assistant to George A. Archer and John W. Daniels and later became the chairman of the board of ADM.

The first fifty years signaled a time of new growth, ingenuity, promise and determination. However, these first fifty years were due to the commitment of some key individuals.

SAM MAIRS

A year after John Daniels started the Daniels Linseed Company, he and George Archer decided they needed a bookkeeper for their growing business. The First National Bank in St. Paul recommended a young man of twenty, a student at the University of Minnesota named Samuel Mairs.

Now that young bookkeeper who began his career on June 1, 1903, is chairman of the board of ADM. He has served as secretary, vice president and executive vice president through his long career of forty-nine years with the Company.

Sam Mairs was born on August 26, 1879, in Hastings, Minnesota. He settled in St. Paul in 1892 so this year is a golden anniversary for him, too.

Sam bicycled from home to work each day back in the early years of the century. He was devoted to George Archer and John Daniels and says today how very helpful and kind both men were: it was like having two fathers, Sam recalls.

The hours that Sam does not spend at his desk today, he's most likely hunting – or curling. In fact, Sam Mairs is a veteran Twin Cities curling champion. His two sons, George, Minneapolis, and Robert, Los Angeles, are both with ADM.

So Sam's "first fifty" is also the "first fifty," career-wise, for Sam Mairs, a living symbol of progress in industry.

T. L. DANIELS

Business, literature, and the arts, if it existed, would be a degree for which T. L. Daniels could well qualify. As president of ADM, he has had a life-long background for the widely diversified business he heads. He was, like George M. Cohan, "born on the Fourth of July" in 1892 in Piqua, Ohio. He came west, from Cleveland to Minneapolis, with his family at the age of ten. His first position in the business that his father founded was as assistant treasurer, then vice president, executive vice president and finally the top position in 1947.

He acquired a wider and international business background during the twenties when he served as secretary to the American embassies in Brussels, Rio and Rome. Experience in leadership he acquired during World War I when he was a major in the U.S. Air Service Reserve Corps – and during World War II, as chief of the fats and oils division of the War Production Board and the War Food Administration.

Now joining the business operation of ADM are his sons, Forrest and John.

Mr. Daniels' interest in literature may have been fostered by his friendship with a shy, quiet young man with whom he attended classes at St. Paul Academy. The young man's name was F. Scott Fitzgerald. T. L. Daniels kept up with Scott's career during the twenties: in fact, he took the original manuscript of "Tender Is the Night" to Fitzgerald's publishers, Charles Scribner's and Sons, in New York.

ADM's president finds leisure pleasure in "the arts," too. His musical interests were well established through personal contacts in this field during his college days at Yale, where he was a member of Phi Beta Kappa and sang with Cole Porter's Whiffenpoof chorus. He carries his musical and artistic interests today through his directorship in the Orchestral Association of Minneapolis and as vice president of the Minneapolis Society of Fine Arts and also by following the career of his son, David, who is presently playing a leading role in "Call Me Madam."

The cultural, business and civic accomplishments of T. L. Daniels have long caused the Northwest to regard him as a leading citizen and an outstanding authority in his field. Just recently, the Minneapolis Sunday Tribune carried a thumbnail biography and picture of ADM's president, naming him an outstanding "Man of Minnesota."

GEORGE A. ARCHER

George Archer, one of the most highly respected men in the linseed oil industry and a pioneer in the field, was born in Dayton, Ohio, September 29, 1850, and maintained a keen interest in the affairs of the concern he helped found until his death at age eighty-two. George Archer started his career in 1868 with the firm Clegg, Wood & Co. founded by his uncle, Joseph Clegg, and his father, William Shreve Archer in 1844.

Then as the flax crop moved west – so did George Archer. He went first to Yankton, South Dakota, then to St. Paul where his enthusiasm for the opportunities awaiting young men in the linseed oil business caused him to write John Daniels in Cleveland urging him to join him.

George Archer had all of the courage, energy and ambition necessary for a pioneer. Trade papers the country over expressed their admiration and respect for his "many sterling qualities."

His advice and kindly counsel were widely sought and his genial, keen face framed by his white hair and trim white mustache was a familiar and welcome sight in the ADM office even when he reached his eighties.

1902–1931 1911–1947

JOHN W. DANIELS

John W. Daniels, first president of ADM, was the man who took a risk and came west from Cleveland in 1902 and lived to see his company grow and expand to an extent he may have thought a mere dream fifty years ago.

John Daniels was born in Piqua, Ohio, on February 23, 1857, and entered the linseed oil business with the firm of William P. Orr and Louis Leonard in 1879. His Daniels Linseed Company, founded on September 30, 1902, was the parent organization of ADM. John Daniels lived his business during office hours and many extra hours, besides. One story his friend L. M. Leffingwell tells about him occurred one late fall day at the Minneapolis Grain Exchange. L. M. Leffingwell and John Daniels walked in, ready to purchase flaxseed, but the place was deserted: they were completely alone. Probably because it was Thanksgiving Day and the two men, so intent on business, had overlooked the holiday.

But John Daniels was not always completely lost in business affairs. He was extremely interested in art and made several trips to Europe to study collections of paintings in noted galleries. In 1927, he gave a Sir Joshua Reynolds portrait to the Minneapolis Institute of the Arts. And perhaps Minnesota winters weren't too unpleasant for him, for he was an ardent ice-skating fan.

Like George Archer, he was widely recognized as an authority in the linseed oil industry, a man noted for his spirit of friendliness and interest in his company until his death at the age of seventy-four in June, 1931.

SHREVE M. ARCHER

ADM's man of the twenties and thirties, Shreve M. Archer, was president through a great period in Company history. He was born on his father's birthday, September 29, 1888 at Yankton, South Dakota and like his contemporary, T.L. Daniels, attended St. Paul Academy and Yale University. Shreve Archer became vice president of the Company in 1923 and president one year later. He held this position for twenty-three years—until his sudden death in 1947.

Shreve Archer was at the peak of his career in the fabulous twenties. Stories about his life and interests are typical of the times in which he lived. During the period of gansterism and lawlessness in St. Paul, his aid to the St. Paul police department was invaluable. Shreve's favorite leisure activity was hunting and he owned one of the finest gun collections in the country---though it was his habit to give a gun to anyone who particularly admired it. He contributed numerous rifles and guns to the police department and one day, when a police officer admired Shreve's new 16 cylinder Cadillac, he immediately turned the car over to the man for him to use as a "crime chaser." Other of his weapons and field glasses were turned over to the FBI arsenal.

Shreve Archer was also a pioneer in aviation. He was intensely interested in the development of Northwest Airlines and was president of the organization at a time when it operated "new, modern 8-passenger planes that might possibly reach a speed of 185 miles per hour."

And not only from his gun collection did Shreve Archer give freely. He was known throughout the Twin Cities for his generosity and help—most often given anonymously.

He carried on his executive position with a wide background for it. He represented the third generation of his family in the linseed oil business. His grandfather, William Shreve Archer, was a pioneer in the field; his father, George, was a founder of ADM; then Shreve and today, Shreve M. Archer represents the third generation active in carrying on the business activities of the Company.

COMPANY FOUNDERS

The biographies of our Company founders were written in celebration of our Company's 50th Anniversary in 1952.

* denotes time with Company

President Richard Nixon
1972

Senator Hubert Humphrey

President John F. Kennedy 1960

President Boris Yeltsin 1989

President Lyndon B. Johnson 1964

President Ronald Reagan 1988

President Fidel Castro 1996

ADM

President Gorbachev 1985

Patriarch Alexy II - 1993

President George Bush 1990

President and Mrs. Jimmy Carter 1980

Mother Teresa and Sandy McMurtrie 1995

President Harry S. Truman - Ivrey Andreas 1945

Dwayne O. Andreas

Dwayne O. Andreas' roots are planted deep in the fertile soil of the nation's heartland. Born in Worthington, Minnesota, in 1918, Andreas moved with his family to a farm in Iowa when he was less than a year old. There, with his parents Reuben and Lydia and his six siblings, he learned how to work hard, rising at 4:30 a.m. to feed the family's chickens and pigs and do other chores on the farm. His Mennonite parents instilled in him a strong sense of discipline, as well as a dependence on the land. After attending public school, graduating from high school in three years and briefly studying for the ministry at Wheaton College in Illinois, Andreas rejoined his father and brothers to sell grain and feed products for his family's company, Honeymead Products. In a harbinger of things to come at ADM, Andreas expanded the scope of his family's business based on what he learned from three mentors who taught him about soybeans, grain and oilseeds.

After being drafted to serve in World War II in 1944, Andreas, who had sold most of his family's company's assets to Cargill before leaving for duty, returned to work for Cargill as vice president of oilseed processing, a position he held for seven years. Long before globalization became the buzzword it is today, Andreas was looking for new markets here and abroad for farmer's products. He left Cargill and returned to what was left of his family's company, successfully growing it until he consolidated it with Archer Daniels Midland in 1965 after the principal owner of the Company, Shreve Archer, died unexpectedly. Within five years, Andreas became chairman and chief executive officer.

ADM's transformation from a regional grain processor to a global agribusiness giant can largely be attributed to the vision and efforts of Dwayne Andreas. When Andreas assumed control of ADM, the Company had 3,000 employees and a net worth of approximately $78 million. By the time he retired in 1999, ADM had about 23,000 employees and a market value that exceeded $10 billion – 128 times the amount it was in 1970.

In addition to the financial success of ADM, some of Andreas' greatest achievements came from helping to feed hungry people throughout the world.

Andreas devoted his time and business skills to help forge political initiatives to provide food for the hungry. In the 1950s, he worked to build bipartisan support in Congress for Public Law 480, which allowed the government to sell food to poor countries for local currency and to lend the local currency back to the countries to increase food supplies.

In the late 1960's, Andreas worked with Senators Bob Dole and Hubert Humphrey to integrate the federal Food Stamp Program into the national economic system. Later, Andreas advocated an International Food Stamp Program to help provide food to people in impoverished Third World countries.

Besides his work to help feed the world, Andreas donated generously to many other charitable causes through his family's foundation, the Andreas Foundation, which he helped establish nearly fifty years ago. Over the years, the foundation has supported churches, educational institutions and programs to provide food to the needy.

In a fitting tribute to his character and accomplishments, Andreas received the Horatio Alger Award in 1994. For more than a half-century, the Horatio Alger Association has paid tribute to the simple but commanding values and beliefs of dedication, purpose and perseverance by recognizing the lives of Americans who not only exemplify this heritage but are committed to sharing a message of hope and encouragement with young people.

While some executives work their careers to get a gold Rolex watch, Andreas built a gold Rolodex, counting among his friends and associates world leaders such as President Ronald Reagan, Mikhail Gorbachev, Fidel Castro, Mother Teresa and many others. He did much for ADM, Decatur and the world and continues to do more in his retirement and in his role as ADM's chairman emeritus.

THE 1950'S — NEW HORIZONS

Thomas L. Daniels, ADM's third president, successfully maintained the Company's tradition of growth and continued to broaden its horizons.

The W. J. Small Company, one of the nation's largest processors of dehydrated alfalfa meal, was acquired in 1951, giving ADM alfalfa processing plants in several mid- and southwestern states. Although alfalfa processing was a new field for ADM, it was closely allied to the Company's agricultural operations since alfalfa was an important ingredient in formula feeds, especially those for livestock and poultry. The facilities of W. J. Small consisted of fifty-six units located in ten states and included harvesting equipment, dehydration and blending plants, control laboratories, warehouses, cold storage plants and an interest in a chlorophyll plant, which was sold a few years later.

ADM introduced new methods of processing and storing, including shaping meal into pellets, which made meal less dusty and easier to handle in bulk. Also, inert gas storage facilities at Schuyler, Nebraska, and Topeka and Marysville, Kansas, enabled ADM to preserve ninety to ninety-five percent of the vitamin A or carotene content of its meal compared to the fifty-five percent made possible by the cold storage method.

One of ADM's chief construction projects during the post-war period was a new plant at Mankato, Minnesota, designed around a solvent extraction unit built primarily for processing flaxseed but convertible to soybean processing. The plant was conveniently located for processing both the Minnesota crop and that of northern Iowa. But even more important in the choice of the site was the fact that ADM already had a formula feed mill there. The solvent extraction plant was built adjacent to the feed mill so that meal could travel by conveyor belt from the extraction unit to the feed plant.

Though a great majority of the expansion during this period was in the form of new construction, research and development continued to play a key role at ADM. In 1951, ADM built a product development plant in Minneapolis that could process, on a small scale, all types of oils and fatty acids and could perform any of ADM's manufacturing operations except extracting oil. This pilot plant, operated by the research department, was an important aid in the development of new products because it provided an intermediate step between the laboratory and the manufacturing plant. At the plant, production could be tested under conditions similar to large-scale manufacturing, and processing techniques could be perfected before production started.

Research was achieving remarkable things for ADM. Because of research, it became possible to produce odorless paints with chemically modified marine oils. Thanks to research, soybean oil, once unpalatable, had become the leading edible oil. Its drying qualities were also improved due to research so that it ranked second only to linseed. And in another testament to the value of research that went right to the bottom line, by 1956, of the nine hundred products ADM offered, sixty-five percent were less than ten years old.

The new products furthered the program of diversification that made such a major contribution toward stabilizing earnings. They were also of prime importance in keeping ADM abreast of the many technological advances of the 1950's, which impacted how the Company marketed its products. In just one example, linseed oil consumption changed radically when paints using little or no drying oil were introduced. In response, ADM research countered with a new type of water emulsion paint vehicle, which offered many advantages over synthetic rubber paints. Other contributions by ADM's research staff during this period included chemically modified starchy flours, thermo-setting resins and new feed formulations.

While agricultural raw materials remained of primary concern, research keyed to chemical processing took on added importance. The industrial cereals division, started in 1947, provided a completely new market for cereal products at a time when conditions in the milling industry were unfavorable. There was a remarkable growth in the sale of these products, developed through research into chemical processing, that used cereals in entirely new ways such as in dynamite, powdered hand soaps, oil well drilling adjuncts and dry cereal binders used with core oil.

The Company's 1954 purchase of the resin division of U.S. Industrial Chemicals Corporation from National Distillers Products Corporation served to reinforce

ADM's long-term objectives. The purchase included inventories, formulations, trademarks and plants at Newark, New Jersey, and Pensacola, Florida. The 150 basic products manufactured at Newark included alkyd and polyester resins and chemically modified oils, used in the protective coatings industry as ingredients in paints, enamels, varnishes and lacquers.

U.S. Industrial Chemicals Corporation also was an importer of the natural resins used in printing inks, nitrocellulose lacquers and other protective coatings. It was best known, however, as one of the leading producers of alkyd resins, which were the basic materials for synthetic industrial enamels, adhesives and allied products.

The purchase enabled ADM to offer the paint industry a complete line of resins, manufactured at five different locations. Also, the operations of ADM's less efficient Edgewater plant were gradually transferred to Newark. The research department benefited, as the Newark plant contained a research laboratory – a very valuable supplement to ADM facilities.

In addition to furthering ADM's diversification, the purchase offered other applications for ADM products, a welcome development in 1954 at a time when marketing conditions for flaxseed and soybeans were unfavorable. Alkyd resins called for glycerin, fatty acids and linseed and soybean oils. During the first year of the purchase of the resin division of U.S. Industrial Chemicals, the new resins consumed more than nine million pounds of these ADM products.

In 1956, in another move aimed at strengthening ADM's market position in alkyd resins, ADM bought from General Electric Company – one of the oldest producers of alkyd resins – the inventories, equipment, formulations and manufacturing specifications from GE's plant at Schenectady, New York.

Purchase of the GE resin operations took ADM even further into the plastics field. Polyesters, basically alkyd resins, were used with glass fiber in matting, cloth and other forms to produce the reinforced plastics whose strength made them adaptable for many specialized purchases.

ADM created an application for vinyl and polyester resins that used their particular qualities to great advantage. With the ADM Freight Liner System for upgrading boxcars, repairs that used to take days could be done in hours at a fraction of the cost, with quick-drying liquid plastics and specially woven glass cloth.

As the broad pattern of the future of ADM began to take shape in the mid-1950's, management turned to new methods of guiding the growth in the desired directions. A development department was established in 1955 to assist in locating and evaluating new products and new markets as well as potential acquisitions. The Company's traditional production-oriented operations turned toward what was then a relatively new concept – marketing.

The search for new products, new markets and new opportunities for growth led ADM to establish an international division in 1955. Just eighteen months after it was organized, the international division was selling ADM products in fifty-one foreign countries, setting the stage for how this began ADM's efforts to open foreign markets to American agricultural products.

Further foreign expansion came rapidly. A formula feed plant was built at Mexico City in 1956. ADM began operation of a land-based whaling station at Paita, Peru, in 1957, an operation that ended in the early 1970s. Interests were purchased in a resins and plastics company in the Netherlands and in a fats and oils processing company in Spain. A chemical company was set up in Belgium and a resin company in West Germany.

In 1958, Thomas L. Daniels, while continuing in his role as chairman, turned the management of ADM over to his son, John H. Daniels, who was elected president. John H. Daniels knew most of the Company's operations firsthand, having begun in sales and worked his way through various procurement and production positions to manage a division prior to his election to the presidency.

The 1960's — Challenges and Changes

By this point, ADM was sending products all over the U.S. by rail and tank trucks and vans and by water in river barges and Great Lakes vessels. Ocean freighters carried ADM products to other continents. Only a few products appeared in the retail market and only one, Archer Polmer-ik Linseed Oil, had national distribution. Consequently, the general public was not yet aware that ADM supplied materials to every major manufacturing industry in the country and was the largest processor in such varied fields as linseed oil, marine oil, paint vehicles, core oils, linseed oil meal, soy flour and flax fiber.

Just over fifty years had passed since the Daniels Linseed Company began with only two products, linseed oil and linseed cake. By 1960, ADM marketed more than nine hundred products. The single mill had expanded into 148 plants and elevators – a vast industrial organization operating in twenty-one states and Canada, with three foreign subsidiaries, a daily capacity in the oil mills of more than 100,000 bushels, and in the flour mills 36,000 hundredweight of flour and semolina, with elevators that could store seventy-four million bushels of grain. The mere handful of employees had grown to almost five thousand, and more than 6,200 stockholders owned shares in ADM, which had grown from a $125,000 initial investment to a company with a net worth of $94,000,000.

The business had succeeded beyond all expectations because it had been managed with foresight and with courage. Over the years the Company had demonstrated its ability to meet the challenge of changing

situations and changing needs, a quality that would be as vital in the future as it had been in the past. With the world as its market, the question now before the Company's leaders was where to turn next.

Studying market trends, growth potential and return on investment, ADM began the 1960's by disposing of a small group of country elevators in Minnesota, as well as a Minneapolis oilseed processing plant. ADM also shut down its equipment division, sold its interest in Applied Radiation Corporation, which it had made when it appeared that radiation had promise as a means of food preservation, and got out of the formula feed business.

At the same time, ADM began construction of a chemical center in Peoria, Illinois, and a new research laboratory in Bloomington, Minnesota.

As plans moved ahead for expansion in the agricultural area, another segment of ADM's business that took on increasing importance was in transportation and distribution. If ADM wanted to grow, it needed to get even better at transporting crops from the fields to the processing plants to customers.

To achieve this, ADM began to assemble what would one day become one of the world's largest transportation and grain storage network of barges, trucks, rail cars, rowboats and grain elevators. This extensive grain origination and product network delivery would enable ADM to transport its raw materials and market its products effectively, with superior logistics for its customers. Customers were coming to ADM for

one-stop shopping, with the goal of dramatically reducing the complexities in dealing with multiple vendors. By building a first class transportation and distribution network, ADM was becoming a key asset for its customers, providing timely and reliable service with superior quality control.

With that in mind, ADM increased its transportation capabilities with a number of important decisions. In a 1963 joint venture with Garnac Company of New York, ADM opened a grain export terminal at Destrehan, Louisiana. The Destrehan terminal provided ADM with a direct outlet on the Gulf Coast, from which fifty percent of the nation's grain export was shipped to foreign markets. It also tied in with the Midwestern terminal elevators on the Mississippi and Illinois Rivers that ADM had purchased from the Norris Grain Company the prior year and with the Company's other terminals located in the mid-continent grain producing area. ADM also had deep-water grain export terminals on the Pacific Coast and at Superior, Wisconsin, at the head of the Great Lakes-St. Lawrence Seaway.

With world demand for food increasing, ADM began to expand its facilities for producing food products, especially soybean products. In 1965, the Company leased a soybean plant at Bloomington, Illinois, and acquired another at Galesburg, Illinois. That same year, ADM began expansion of the soybean oil refinery at Decatur, Illinois, and installed hydrogenation equipment there to upgrade soybean oils for food. The next year, the Company opened a plant to produce textured vegetable protein (TVP®) at the Decatur soybean complex. TVP was developed in ADM's research laboratories as an economical source of nutritious protein that could be flavored and formed to resemble meats and other foods. In 1966, ADM also announced plans to open a new soybean processing plant and soybean oil refinery at Lincoln, Nebraska.

By 1967, ADM had proven its ability to meet changing conditions, to develop new products, to satisfy new needs and to open new markets at home and abroad. These qualities marked ADM's growth through its first sixty-five years. They were also amply demonstrated when the Company decided to sell its chemical operations and concentrate exclusively on agricultural and food fields. Although ADM Chemicals had made steady progress, two trends were apparent to management. The first was the movement of the chemical industry from the naturally based raw materials used by ADM in the manufacture of its chemicals to petroleum-based materials. The second was the almost unlimited potential for growth in agricultural processing and food ingredient manufacturing as the world demand for food increased.

In April of 1967, ADM sold its entire chemical group to Ashland Oil & Refining Company. At about the same time, the Company decided to devote its full resources to profitable areas of growth in the agricultural processing business. This decision prompted the sale of the dehydrated alfalfa division to Kansas

Nebraska Natural Gas Company and the completion of a soybean oil refining and hydrogenation plant in Decatur, Illinois, for producing refined and hardened oils for the food industry, primarily for use in margarine, shortenings, cooking and salad oils. This meant ADM doubled and subsequently redoubled its capacity for producing TVP.

Even before the sale of the chemical group for sixty-five million dollars, ADM had invested or committed twenty-five million dollars for acquisitions and new facilities to expand its agricultural processing and marketing operations. In another important investment, ADM purchased a fleet of thirty barges to transport agricultural products economically on the Mid-America Waterways System.

On February 2, 1968, Erwin A. Olson retired as chairman of the board after twenty-six years with ADM. John H. Daniels was elected to succeed him, and Lowell W. Andreas was named president.

In 1969, ADM moved its corporate offices and research laboratory to Decatur, Illinois, and the headquarters of the flour division to Kansas City, Missouri. These moves were extremely significant because they helped ADM become more closely aligned with the source of raw materials that made up its domestic production and set the stage for further expansion, not just on a national stage, but on an international one as well.

But like any great company, if ADM were going to grow on a worldwide level and grow rapidly, it would need a visionary leader capable of taking it there, a leader who would not only know ADM and the industry, but would also know the world and where it was heading. Dwayne O. Andreas, who had joined ADM in 1966 at the invitation of Shreve M. Archer and who considered food to be far and away the most important business in the world, was that visionary leader.

Named chief executive in 1970, Dwayne Andreas was elevated to the chairmanship in 1972 when John H. Daniels left the Company to become chairman of Independent Bancorporation, Minneapolis. Dwayne Andreas envisioned turning ADM from a mostly regional, medium-sized processor of corn and soybeans into an agribusiness involved in the buying, processing and marketing of a wide variety of agricultural products, which it would sell and deliver around the world.

In the decades to follow, ADM turned from a one hundred-million-dollar company into a company worth more than $6.5 billion.

PRESIDENT • CHAIRMAN

JOHN W. DANIELS
President: 1902 – 1924
Chairman: 1924 – 1931

GEORGE A. ARCHER
Chairman: 1931 – 1932

SHREVE M. ARCHER
President: 1924 – 1947

LOWELL W. ANDREAS
President: 1968 – 1972

DONALD B. WALKER
President: 1972 – 1975
Vice Chairman: 1975 – 1977

JAMES R. RANDALL
President: 1975 – 1997

SAMUEL MAIRS

Chairman: 1947 – 1955

THOMAS L. DANIELS

President: 1947 – 1958

Chairman: 1958 – 1964

JOHN H. DANIELS

President: 1958 – 1968

Chairman: 1968 – 1972

ERWIN A. OLSON

Chairman: 1965 – 1968

DWAYNE O. ANDREAS

Chief Executive: 1970 – 1972

Chairman and Chief Executive:

1972 – 1999

Chairman Emeritus: 1999 –

G. ALLEN ANDREAS

President and Chief Executive:

1997 – 1999

Chairman and Chief Executive:

1999 –

JOHN D. MCNAMARA

President: 1999 – 2001

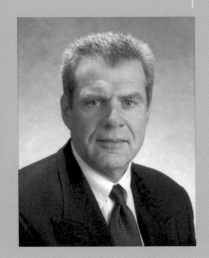

PAUL B. MULHOLLEM

President: 2001 –

THE 1970'S – CORN TAKES CENTER STAGE

With the relocation of ADM's headquarters and research facilities to Decatur, ADM was now virtually at the center of the nation's corn- and soybean-growing acreage. And with ADM International moving its headquarters to Brussels, Belgium, and the newly named president of ADM International, A. J. Langsdorf, joining Dwayne Andreas in the executive suite, ADM was poised to assert its agricultural leadership on the global stage.

To Dwayne Andreas, when it concerned agriculture, evangelizing abroad was not foreign territory. As early as 1952, at the age of thirty-four, Andreas went to Moscow as a vice president for Cargill to interest the Soviet Union in buying American vegetable oils. This began a relationship he would nurture in the decades to follow on behalf of ADM and American farmers. It also began a practice he would continue and eventually take to other countries and continents.

Just as Mr. Archer and Mr. Daniels were pioneers when they founded ADM, in Dwayne Andreas' twenty-nine years at the helm of ADM, he was a pioneer in discovering innovative ways to turn American bounty into a product useable to consumers. He looked at starch, oil and gluten and saw opportunities to turn them into new products, in new ways. Most importantly, not only was this an accurate description of Dwayne Andreas, it was an accurate description of ADM as a whole. In addition to the influence ADM had on the prices of crops, one of ADM's biggest impacts was in developing new uses and international markets for U.S. agricultural products.

Beginning with the early 1970's, two of ADM's biggest developments involved corn, specifically high fructose corn syrup (HFCS), followed later by ethanol.

Historically, corn byproducts had been produced in large volumes, but had yielded low returns. In 1969, a relatively new technology, wet corn milling, which had been developed and perfected in Japan, promised to transform the reliable corn crop and deliver more financially rewarding results. With wet corn milling, an enzyme was applied to cornstarch, converting dextrose into highly sweetened fructose. When ADM first began to commercialize the process, its improved sweeteners worked well in canned and baked products, but the ultimate customer, the cola industry, was not yet convinced there could be an adequate substitute for sugar.

Then, in 1971, sugar prices skyrocketed, causing sugar users to seek out more stable, dependable sources of sweeteners. Sensing a burgeoning trend and therefore an opportunity in high fructose corn syrup, ADM acquired a fifty percent interest – eighty-three percent by year-end – in Corn Sweeteners, Inc., a wet corn milling plant in Cedar Rapids, Iowa. Additionally, the Company acquired Union Starch, a subsidiary of Miles Laboratories' Granite City, Illinois, wet corn-milling operations, to operate as part of Corn Sweeteners. Finally, with the goal of significantly lowering costs and improving quality, ADM announced plans to construct a new fifty-million-dollar dextrose facility at the site of Corn Sweeteners' Cedar Rapids plant. About the same time, while ADM was developing sugar substitutes, the Company rounded out its line of sweeteners by acquiring the Supreme Sugar Company in Louisiana.

Together with further research into HFCS applications, these developments enabled ADM to sell products from wet corn milling to a wide variety of food industries, including confectionery, bakery and cereal, canning and preserves and beverages. Mountain Dew and Welch's Sparkling Grape Soda were the first companies to come around, followed by Coca-Cola and Pepsi-Cola, as well as industrial markets such as the paper, paperboard and corrugating industries.

In 1972, Lowell W. Andreas resigned as president to become chairman of ADM's newly formed management committee, which was responsible for planning and controlling major activities of ADM and its various subsidiaries. Donald B. Walker, former executive vice president, was elected president.

ADM made another significant move at this time, acquiring the assets of companies owned by John Vanier at Salinas, Kansas. In consumer product areas, Vanier manufactured and marketed a variety of retail consumer-packaged food products sold primarily under Gooch Food labels. The new operations afforded ADM a significant market for its meat analog, TVP.

Ten years after introducing TVP, ADM introduced a second generation of TVP containing seventy percent protein. The Company also kept growing, both domestically and internationally, through acquisitions including soybean plants in Holland and Brazil; Tabor Grain, which included Coeval, Miller Hauling and Tabor Milling; the Havana, Illinois, barge terminal; and Golden Grain and Feeds. ADM also established some new entities, including the ADMIC and Agrinational Offshore Insurance Companies, ADM Leasco, ADM Trucking and ADM Truck Lease.

As they had in the past, farmers would count on ADM, the bridge between two giant industries – agriculture and food – to play a substantial role in determining the future of agriculture. Why was ADM so critical? At this point, ADM was transforming the harvests from farmland into flours for baked goods and pastas, into vegetable oils and proteins, into sweeteners, into malt, into potable alcohol and into animal feeds that eventually became meat and dairy products. In short, the ingredients ADM supplied to the food industry each year were processed into a myriad of consumer foods with a retail value of thirty billion dollars.

THE 1980's – MORE CORN-FUELED GROWTH

By 1980, every minute of the day, ADM's global facilities were processing the equivalent of sixty football fields' worth of wheat, oats, rice, barley, corn, sorghum, soybeans and sunflowers. As a result, almost any product, on any shelf, in any grocery store, contained one or even several of the food ingredients made and marketed by ADM.

In ADM, farmers had a partner who wasn't satisfied with being the biggest customer of their raw products, huge crops of corn and soybeans. This partner saw and developed new uses for their products and expanded their markets by bartering and bargaining through barriers to international trade.

As has previously been discussed, some of the best examples of ADM's impact on agriculture during this period could be found in corn. ADM had already developed a market for corn sweeteners with HFCS, causing consumption patterns to drastically change, much to the benefit of the American farmer. In 1980, for example, U.S. per capita consumption of sweeteners was 125 pounds. Of that amount, seventy percent came from sugar and thirty percent from corn. Over time, that would change. By 1997, with ADM leading the way, U.S. per capita sweetener consumption hit

165 pounds, with sixty percent coming from corn and forty percent from sugar.

Besides HFCS, another major contributor to ADM's growth during the late 1970's and 1980's was ethanol. Americans first became aware of ethanol – ethyl alcohol, an ingredient of gasohol, an unleaded alternative fuel — during the energy crisis of the late 1970's. Blending ethanol into gasoline stretches the supply of gas by ten percent. As an added benefit, ethanol provides many important environmental benefits. Gasohol, a mix of ninety percent gasoline and ten percent ethanol, reduces the carbon monoxide in auto exhaust emissions by thirty-three percent.

Dwayne Andreas had been interested in ethanol's potential for decades. Under his direction, ADM invested $13.5 million in a plant that could convert the wastes derived from processing corn into six million gallons of ethanol — two and a half million bushels worth of corn.

Moreover when the 1979 Iranian revolution began and the resulting fuel shortages hit the United States, ADM was ready. The investment paid dividends immediately as almost ten thousand service stations

in the United States were equipped with gasohol pumps within one year. It wasn't easy, as ADM fought a David vs. Goliath battle against the well-heeled petroleum industry, but ADM gained important support from organizations such as the Iowa Corn Promotion Board, the Illinois Corn Growers Association, the Renewable Fuels Association, the National Corn Growers Association and the United States Department of Agriculture. By 1988, 325 million bushels of corn were going into 825 million gallons of ethanol a year, a renewable resource limited only by the number of bushels of corn used to produce it.

Brazil, which imported ten billion dollars worth of petroleum each year and which had a rapidly deteriorating environment in its major cities, jumped into alternative fuels in a big way and also became an important driver of ethanol growth for ADM.

ADM also continued to build market share and capacity through expansion. One major activity involved the acquisition of Clinton Corn Processing from Nabisco in 1982. The company had been an early innovator in developing the technology for HFCS and when ADM purchased it, ADM became the largest corn processor in the world in only twelve short years. ADM had also purchased the Hiram Walker Distillery at Peoria, Illinois, in 1980 and had converted it into an ethanol producing facility.

Another notable acquisition was in 1983, when ADM bought a fifty percent share in Alfred C. Toepfer International, a German trading firm in Hamburg. From its offices in fifty countries, Toepfer grossed eight billion dollars in sales and handled thirty million tons of assorted commodities such as wheat, corn, barley and soybeans each year. The Toepfer acquisition strengthened ADM's grain trading network, particularly in key overseas markets like Europe, South America and the Far East.

While HFCS and ethanol were consuming billions of bushels of corn and helping to support the price of corn, ADM still supported the soybean market as well, processing beans and creating new products needed around the world. After years of research, ADM discovered how to make a product from soy isolate proteins blended with corn sweeteners for carbohydrates and vegetable oil as a fat source. The use of soy as a protein source was becoming very important for ADM and continued ADM's practice of pioneering

the development of healthier foods for healthier diets. In soy, consumers were getting a high quality, inexpensive protein source with great nutritional value. They were also getting more food choices – and, as always, farmers were getting even greater markets for their products.

During the early eighties, the first contract ever with Exportkhleb was signed on a napkin during a dinner in the National Hotel in Moscow. The contract was for 25,000 tons of corn from Tabor.

ROUNDUP "WATCH YOUR STEP!"

THINK SAFETY!

1. RECOGNIZE THE STORY

2. GET THE FACTS

3. PICTURE THE PRODUCT

4. RETAKES FOR ACCURACY

5. FIRST DRAFT

6. CHECK WITH RESEARCH

7. CHECK WITH SALES

8. RETAKES FOR ACCURACY

9. FINAL DRAFT

10. RELEASE FOR PUBLICATION

For Immediate Release
the ADM 10-Point Publicity Plan

Artwork is taken from Archer newsletters in the late 1940s through the early 1960s.

43

THE 1990'S – FEEDING THE WORLD

By 1990, ADM was on its way to becoming the undisputed market leader in the global agricultural processing industry with annual revenues of over eight billion dollars, a net income of close to five hundred million dollars and operations in sixty countries. In the United States alone, close to ten thousand employees in 118 processing plants in twenty-nine states sold, stored and shipped more than seventy-five million tons of corn, soybeans, wheat and other commodities each year. ADM was buying five million bushels of grain and oilseeds a day (and selling a thousand tons per day of ingredients for ready-to-eat soy products) and had a storage capacity of two hundred million bushels in its grain elevators.

Prior to the 1990's, ADM had expanded across Europe and the Eastern Bloc, but it was in South America and Asia Pacific where ADM would achieve its next big growth story.

Brazil was becoming a major producer and exporter of agricultural products, particularly soybeans. In response to this growth of a new supply of oilseeds, ADM increased its elevator storage capacity and processing network by moving aggressively into the South American market. One key acquisition in this

area was Glencore's Brazilian Grain, which included a head office in São Paulo, approximately thirty-three grain elevators and a fertilizer processing plant. Another was the acquisition of SARTCO Ltd., a Brazilian grain and transportation business with seventeen towboats and sixty-one barges on the Tiete and Parana rivers.

In China, where soybeans had first been discovered, Dwayne Andreas had made efforts to become a large-scale buyer of the isolated country's surplus soybeans as early as 1966. With the advent of the 1990's and a more dynamic economic policy in China, the Chinese economy was growing. As a result of this growth, per capita income in the country was also rising, allowing individual Chinese to improve the quality of their diets and add more protein to their daily meals. In 2000, ADM established five new crushing plants in China to meet this growing need.

ADM also entered the cocoa business in the late 1990's, purchasing the cocoa operations of W. R. Grace. The acquisition was a natural fit for ADM as many cocoa buyers were also large purchasers of flour, sweeteners and emulsifiers made by other ADM divisions. With the acquisition, ADM brought technical

expertise in agriculture and distribution, as well as a high degree of professional management and stability.

With the close of the decade, an era passed at ADM as Dwayne Andreas, after twenty-nine years at the helm, stepped down as chairman of the board. While he would remain on the board serving as chairman emeritus, he passed control and strategic direction of the Company to his nephew, G. Allen Andreas, in 1997. Prior to assuming the CEO position, Allen Andreas had directed ADM's expansion in Europe and South America throughout the 1990's. This extensive experience in global agribusiness issues helped to provide him with the insight and vision necessary to lead ADM in the increasingly global agriculture economy of the twenty-first century.

Circa 2002

The Twenty-First Century — from a Quick Glance to a Long View

As Allen Andreas led ADM into the twenty-first century, he identified three trends that would play a major role in ADM's business: increased globalization of the food economy, concerns about health and wellness and an emphasis on natural and renewable resources.

As a truly global company with an efficient matrix of hundreds of facilities in scores of countries, ADM was already at the forefront of these three trends. With the most extensive transportation network in the corporate world, its fleet of trucks, rail cars, barges and ocean-going vessels enabled it to meet the demand for its products anywhere in the world. More importantly, as globalization continued and the world economy grew, the demand for a high-calorie, nutritionally sound diet would expand with it.

The second key to ADM's success would be the increasing concern about health and wellness. Concerns about the nutritional and functional value of food grew in the latter part of the twentieth century, and in all likelihood will continue to grow. ADM has made a commitment to pioneering and developing the nutraceutical industry to meet these needs.

While the world's population grows, the planet's resources remain finite. ADM is a leader in developing renewable, nature-based products to meet the needs of a growing globe. For example, ADM's efforts to expand the market for cleaner-burning renewable ethanol will help to reduce the world's increasing dependence on diminishing oil reserves. The Company's efforts to develop natural forms of plastic derived from soy and industrial solvents based on corn are just two examples of how ADM is working for a cleaner, sustainable future for the planet.

Together with shareholders, suppliers and customers, ADM is poised to lead the world through a new century of innovation and The Nature of What's to Come.

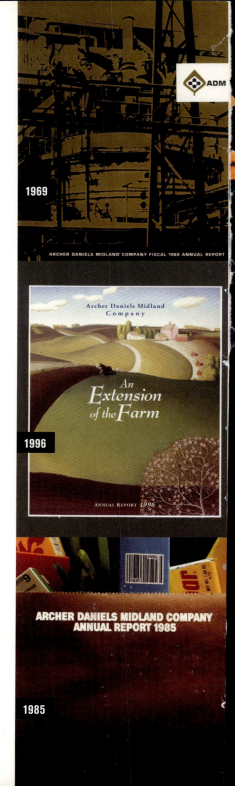

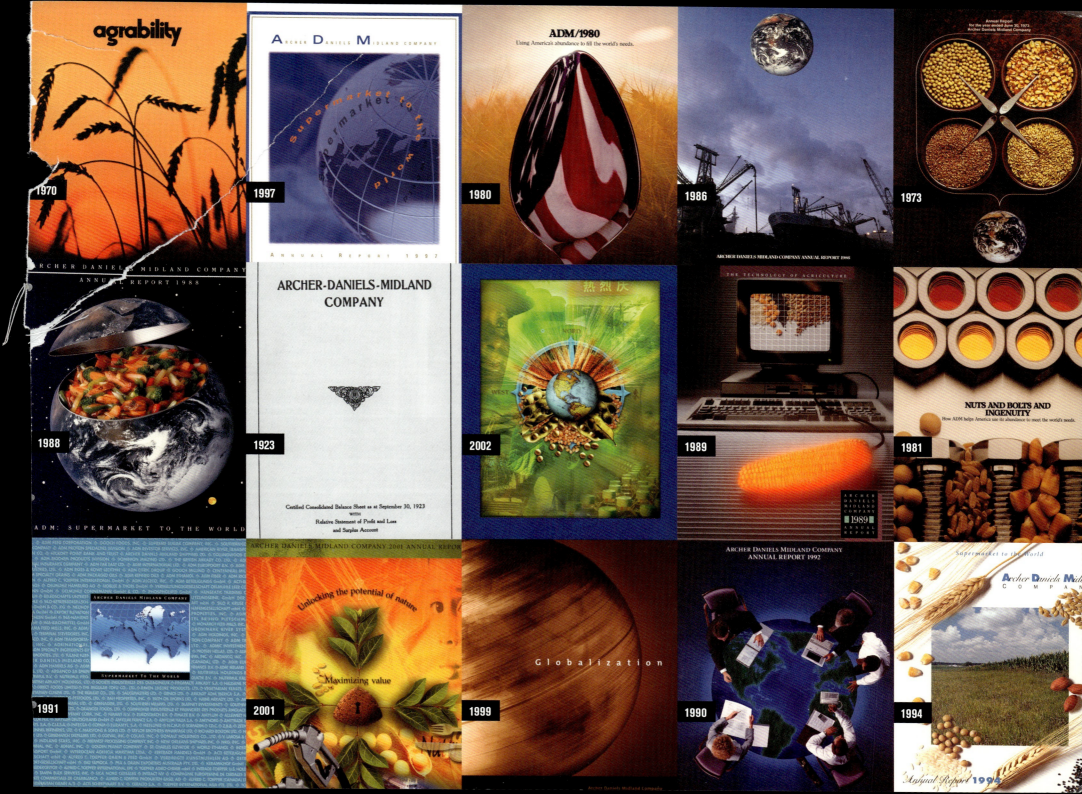

ADM TIMELINE

1900 – 1909

1902 – John W. Daniels founds Daniels Linseed Company in Minneapolis, Minnesota, and is named president.

1903 – George A. Archer joins John W. Daniels in Minneapolis.

1903 – The first bottle of flax linseed oil is made at the Archer-Daniels Mill on February 17.

1905 – The Company name is changed to the Archer Daniels Linseed Company.

1910 – 1919

1911 – Capitalization reaches $1,000,000.

1914 – The Company's first expansion takes place when a linseed mill is leased in Superior, Wisconsin.

1915 – The Company expands to compete in eastern markets by building a linseed mill and a public grain elevator in Buffalo, New York.

Port Gibson facility, circa between 1882 and 1885.

1920 – 1929

1923 – The Company hires its first chemist for research.

1923 – The Midland Linseed Products Company purchase occurs; the Company's name changes to Archer Daniels Midland Company.

1924 – John W. Daniels leaves his position as president and becomes chairman. Shreve M. Archer is named president.

1925 – The Company builds its first concrete grain elevator in Minneapolis.

1927 – The Armour Grain Company is purchased, forming ADM's Grain division.

1928 – ADM has a record $8.036 per share earnings.

1929 – ADM purchases the Werner G. Smith Company of Cleveland, Ohio, the country's largest manufacturer of core oils.

1929 – ADM starts crushing soybeans in its Toledo and Chicago plants, becoming a leader in the rapid development of soybeans in the United States.

1929 – ADM acquires the Commander Larabee Corporation, one of the largest flour milling operations in America at the time.

1930 – 1939

1931 – John W. Daniels passes away and George A. Archer is named chairman.

1932 – George Archer passes away. During 1932-1947, ADM president Shreve Archer serves in the capacity of chairman, although he did not have the title.

1933 – ADM begins the manufacturing of formula feeds.

1934 – ADM installs the first continuous solvent extraction unit in the United States at the Chicago plant and begins the solvent extraction of soybeans.

1935 – ADM achieves a record net profit after income tax and depreciation (hereafter referred to as "net earnings") of $2,525,745 dollars.

1939 – ADM begins construction of what was then the world's largest solvent extraction plant at Decatur, Illinois.

1940 – 1949

1940 – New products development through research grows rapidly, turning raw linseed and crude soybean oil into several hundred different products.

1946 – Current assets reach $50,284,312 with sales of $186,255,175.

1947 – Net sales and other operating income increase to $297,429,912 and create record net earnings of $15,673,041. Shareholders' equity rises to $54,748,884.

1947 – Shreve M. Archer passes away and Thomas L. Daniels is elected president. Samuel Mairs is named chairman.

1950 – 1959

Samuel Mairs, chairman of the board, holds a photograph of the original Daniels Linseed facility on ADM's 50th Anniversary.

1952 – The cost of property, plant and equipment is $54,107,838, exceeding $50 million dollars for the first time.

1952 – The number of ADM employees grows to over 5,000.

1954 – ADM purchases the resin division of U.S. Industrial Chemicals, with plants in Newark, New Jersey, and Pensacola, Florida.

1955 – Samuel Mairs passes away. Another chairman will not be named until 1958.

1956 – ADM pays its 100th consecutive quarterly payment, a record of twenty-five years of uninterrupted stock dividends.

1957 – ADM enters the isolated soy protein business.

1958 – T. L. Daniels steps down as president and is elected chairman. John H. Daniels is elected president.

1960 – 1969

1962 – The ADM logo is changed from the Archer yeoman to a logo design meant to represent chemical molecules coming from a natural resource.

1963 – ADM completes its grain export terminal at Destrehan, Louisiana. This is its first direct outlet to the Gulf Coast.

1964 – T. L. Daniels steps down as chairman and Erwin A. Olson is elected as chairman.

1966 – ADM begins producing textured vegetable protein TVP® at the Decatur East Plant.

1967 – Net sales and other operating income increase to $371,625,700 and create net earnings of $4,370,293. Shareholders' equity rises to $91,297,180.

1967 – ADM sells its Chemical Group to Ashland Oil & Refining Company in a refocus on agricultural products.

1967 – ADM purchases a fleet of thirty barges, the start of its transport fleet.

1967 – ADM completes its soybean oil refining and hydrogenation plant in Decatur, Illinois.

1970 – 1979

1968 – Net sales and other operating income decrease to $280,771,608 as net earnings increase to $4,413,558. Shareholders' equity changes to $89,999,809.

1968 – Erwin A. Olson steps down as chairman. John H. Daniels steps down as president and is elected chairman and Lowell W. Andreas is elected president.

1969 – ADM moves its corporate offices and research laboratory to Decatur, Illinois.

1969 – ADM forms its Specialty Division to market a variety of specialty items in the food and industrial areas, including TVP®.

1970 – ADM acquires assets of companies, enabling the Company to return to the mixed feed and dry corn milling businesses.

1970 – Vanier food operations is purchased.

1970 – Dwayne O. Andreas is elected to the position of chief executive.

1971 – ADM acquires an eighty-three percent interest in Corn Sweeteners, Inc., a wet corn milling plant in Cedar Rapids, Iowa.

1972 – Lowell Andreas steps down as president and Donald B. Walker is named his successor. John H. Daniels steps down as chairman and Dwayne Andreas is elected chairman and chief executive.

1972 – ADM forms the American River Transportation Company.

1973 – ADM acquires a fifty percent interest in British Arkady.

1974 – Net sales and other operating income reach $1,551,288,700, creating net earnings of $29,410,385. Shareholders' equity reaches $176,922,649.

1974 – ADM acquires soybean plants in Holland and Brazil, its first processing facilities in Europe and South America.

1975 – Donald Walker steps down as president and is elected vice chairman of the board. James R. Randall is elected president.

1977 – Donald Walker steps down as vice chairman.

1977 – ADM employees number approximately 5,000.

1978 – During the Arab oil embargo, President Carter asks Dwayne Andreas to convert a new beverage alcohol plant into a synfuel plant.

1978 – An ethanol production plant starts up in Decatur.

1979 – Total assets rise to $1,032,523,000.

1979 – ADM Trucking is established.

1980 – 1989

1980 – Net earnings are $115, 958,000 on net sales and other operating income of $2,802,011,000. Shareholders' equity increases to $766,971,000.

1980 – ADM Industrial Oils is established.

1980 – The Peoria, Illinois, ethanol plant is purchased.

1981 – ADM pays its 200th consecutive quarterly payment, a record of fifty years of uninterrupted stock dividends.

1981 – An ethanol production plant starts up in Cedar Rapids, Iowa.

1982 – ADM purchases Clinton, Iowa, ethanol production plant.

1983 – ADM acquires interest in A. C. Toepfer; establishes ADM Asia Pacific Ltd., Hong Kong.

1984 – President Ronald Reagan visits ADM.

1985 – ADM acquires elevators from Growmark and establishes ADM/GROWMARK River Systems, Inc.

1986 – Expansion in Europe: ADM acquires Unilever plants in Hamburg & Spyck, West Germany and Europoort, the Netherlands.

1988 – ADM purchases the soy isolate business from Grain Processing and the sunflower and canola plant at Velva, North Dakota, from Midwest Processing Company, Inc.

1989 – Net earnings are $424,673,000 on net sales and other operating income of $7,928,836,000. Shareholders' equity increases to $3,033,503,000.

1989 – ADM constructs an industrial soy protein facility in Decatur.

1990 – 1999

1990 – The veggie burger is introduced to the U.S. and U.S.S.R. markets.

1991 – ADM enters the citric acid business.

1991 – Walhalla, North Dakota, ethanol plant bought.

1992 – ADM builds pilot plant operations for canola oil-based biodiesel fuel in Leer, Germany.

1992 – Former Soviet President, Mikhail Gorbachev, visits ADM.

1994 – Asian expansion: investments into Wilmar holdings, Singapore, are made with our main JV partner in Asia; first investment into China, East Ocean Oils & Grains (EOGI) in Zhangjiagang, is initiated.

1996 – Net earnings are $695,912,000 on net sales and other operating income of $13,314,049,000. Shareholders' equity increases to $6,144,812,000. Total assets increase to $10,449,869,000.

1996 – ADM builds a new TVP plant at the Europoort facility.

1996 – ADM purchases a twenty-two percent interest in Gruma S.A. de C.V.

2000 —

1997 – James R. Randall retires as president. G. Allen Andreas is named president and chief executive.

1997 – ADM enters the cocoa business.

1997 – Brazilian expansion: ADM acquires Glencore's Brazilian grain operations, including a head office in São Paulo, approximately thirty-three grain elevators and a fertilizer processing plant.

1997 – ADM acquires Moorman Manufacturing Company and subsidiaries.

1998 – Nobel Peace Prizewinner and former Israeli Prime Minister Shimon Peres visits ADM.

1999 – Dwayne Andreas steps down as chief executive and chairman and is named chairman emeritus. G. Allen Andreas steps down as president and is named chairman and chief executive. John D. McNamara is named president.

1999 – ADM Rice, Inc. forms, to be involved in the origination and export trading of rough-paddy rice and milled rice.

2000 – The construction of five new crushing plants in China occurs.

2001 – ADM acquires Doysan Yag Sanayii, a Turkish vegetable oil producer with crushing plant, refinery and packaging operations.

2001 – ADM acquires Aceitiera del Oriente, S.A. (SAO), a Bolivian vegetable oil producer with crushing plant, refinery, packaging operations and grain elevators.

2001 – In April, ADM announces a new corporate logo, tagline and advertising campaign designed to underscore the Company's deep commitment to nature and global agriculture.

2001 – ADM pays its 300th cash dividend and 280th consecutive quarterly payment, a record of seventy years of uninterrupted stock dividends.

2001 – John D. McNamara steps down as president and Paul B. Mulhollem is elected president.

2001 – ADM creates a technology council with P&G Chemicals aimed at developing innovative natural-based products.

2001 – ADM makes history when it becomes the first U.S. company to sign a contract with Cuba since the embargo began nearly forty years ago.

2002 – ADM completes its acquisition of Minnesota Corn Processors, LLC (MCP). With the acquisition, ADM adds corn wet-milling plants located in Marshall, Minnesota, and Columbus, Nebraska.

2002 – Net earnings are $511,093,000 on net sales and other operating income of $23,453,561,000. Shareholders' equity increases to $6,754,821,000 equal to $10.39 per common share. Total assets increase to $15,416,273,000.

2002 – ADM employees grow to over 24,000.

ADM TODAY

When John W. Daniels and George A. Archer rolled up their sleeves and sat across from each other amidst the sound of machinery and the smell of linseed oil in 1902, they could never have imagined what Archer Daniels Midland Company would one day become. Their industriousness and determination formed the culture of ADM. Its heritage dates back one hundred years and the spirit of its founders accompanies ADM into the twenty-first century.

The Archer Daniels Midland Company has entered the new millennium with a heightened sense of commitment, a clear vision of the future and a spirit of openness that will allow us to not simply dream about a better world, but to make meaningful progress in improving the lives of billions of people in every corner of the globe.

Fighting hunger. Cleaning up our planet. Working to improve health. The 24,000 employees of ADM are dedicated to contributing every day, in countless ways, to make these goals a reality.

It is with determination and energy that ADM moves forward to face the challenges of an ever-changing world and to bring passion to embrace great ideas and make them work. And an even stronger resolve to encourage everyone at ADM, in every position and department, to apply their talents, ingenuity and creativity to help successfully carry out its mission.

How, exactly, does ADM see its mission? It is stated here, clearly and concisely. And as employees help plant the seeds for a better future, it defines the essence, purpose and fundamental beliefs of the Archer Daniels Midland Company.

Our Mission

To unlock the potential of nature

to improve the quality of life.

Our Commitment

To make the world a better place by

applying advancements in research

and technology to agriculture.

What We Believe

Our most valuable assets are our people and our customers.

Responsible corporate governance delivers value for our shareholders.

Agriculture is the key to sustainable global growth.

In an innovative, entrepreneurial environment that empowers great ideas.

In the creativity to see, the freedom to develop and the capacity to act.

In integrity and responsiveness in all our interactions.

In profound respect for our environment.

UNLOCKING THE POTENTIAL OF NATURE

Archer Daniels Midland Company is based upon a specific principle: the belief that nature is the only source of renewable, sustainable wealth and value. ADM sees in a single seed not just the beginnings of life, but a storehouse of possibilities, a treasure trove of products and solutions. ADM believes that nature has answers – ADM's job is to discover the secrets it holds and to unlock the potential within.

A century after the Company's founding, ADM has grown to become one of the world's leading processors of corn, soybeans, wheat, cocoa and other crops. It is a global company with facilities and operations in six continents. Yet, for all its size, everything done at ADM begins with the natural, renewable bounty of the world's farms.

ADM is a key link between the farmer and the global marketplace for agricultural products. Through processing, ADM unlocks the value of agricultural commodities by turning the farmer's crops into higher value end products – even as it builds stronger global markets and heightened demand for grains, oilseeds and other raw materials.

Supporting this operation is one of the most vertically integrated agricultural processing infrastructures in the world. With this infrastructure, ADM is able to transport crops from the farmer's field, process them through a global network of plants and then distribute the product directly to consumer goods manufacturers or to supermarket shelves.

1. John H. Daniels and T.L. Daniels.

2. William T. Atkinson was known as the "grandfather of vegetable protein." During the fifties and sixties, Mr. Atkinson discovered a method in order to "puff" soy protein into a meat-like substance, which contained fifty percent protein and fifty percent carbohydrates according to a feature story in the Decatur Herald & Review, November 7, 1995 article.
The contributions of Mr. Atkinson's work were noted by many in the agriculture industry. The photograph was inscribed, "Bill, this lab is a tribute to your great work. Regards, Dwayne."

3. During his tenure in the agriculture industry, Dr. H. H. Schopmeyer acquired over twenty-five patents and a wealth of experience in each of the disciplines of grain processing: production management, research and quality control and manufacturing process design. "Doc," as he was known around ADM, once noted, "Corn syrup is a commodity; our product is conformity."

4. 1962 — Former president of ADM, Mr. Jim Randall (left), pictured at a soybean crushing plant. Mr. Randall retired from the Company in 1997 after twenty-nine years of dedicated service- twenty-two years of which he served as president. At the time of his retirement, Mr. Dwayne Andreas stated, "I have known and worked with Jim Randall since 1948. I consider him to be the industry's greatest innovator. He has played a major role in building ADM's global operating network of processing plants and storage facilities linked by unparalleled world-wide communication and transportation systems."

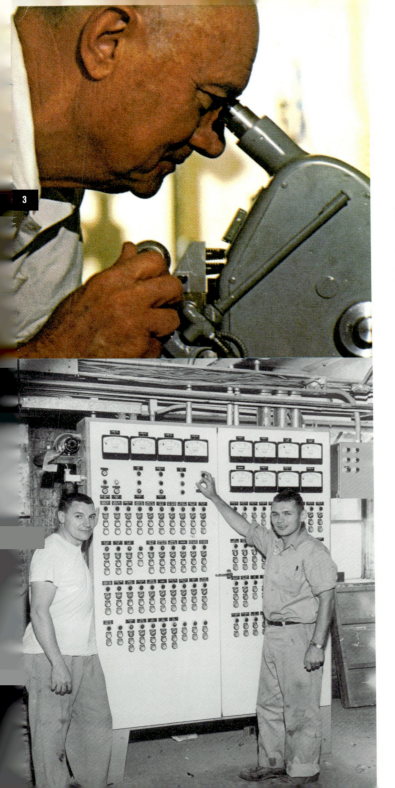

IMPROVING THE QUALITY OF LIFE

Archer Daniels Midland Company believes that nature can be a source of solutions to many of the world's pressing problems. For the last one hundred years, ADM has played a central role in the growth of American agriculture and its amazing achievements in feeding a hungry world. As the world's largest processor of food and animal feed, ADM processes enough food to feed more than 130 million people.

ADM's commitment to improving the quality of life doesn't end with feeding the hungry. Through its processes and plants, ADM transforms nature's bounty into end products that also provide the malnourished with vitally important nutrients that may be missing from their existing diets. Closer to home, ADM provides food manufacturers with the ingredients they need to manufacture better packaged foods -– products that meet the complex and wholesome nutritional profile demanded by today's consumer.

If ample food, adequate nutrition and good health are basic needs, so too are the needs for sustainable sources of energy, industrial chemicals and other products that minimize the impact upon the environment. A leader in renewable fuels as the world's largest producer of ethanol, Archer Daniels Midland

Company continues to pioneer the use of natural resources in place of petrochemicals.

Fuel ethanol is a well-known success story. Made from corn, ethanol is a cleaner burning and renewable automotive fuel and gasoline additive that improves air quality even as it reduces reliance on shrinking global oil reserves. ADM also produces biodiesel – a diesel fuel, made from vegetable oil, that burns cleaner than traditional petroleum products. In addition, ADM produces a number of naturally based industrial products, including a variety of solvents, lubricants and raw materials suitable for the production of biodegradable plastics.

ADM's answers are based on nature, but its products are the result of forward-thinking research and development, hard work and a commitment to providing individually tailored products to meet each customer's unique needs. Working together with customers, ADM is able to provide the world's consumers with food, with feed, with breakthrough industrial products and energy solutions, with answers to tomorrow's problems today.

Oilseed Processing

EXTRACTING FRESH IDEAS

It is well known that Archer Daniels Midland Company is one of the world's largest processors of oilseeds, including soybeans, canola or rapeseeds, flaxseeds, cottonseeds and sunflower seeds. Less well known is how much the tremendous size of its raw material stream allows ADM to accomplish.

These key agricultural commodities are essential components of many basic foods, food ingredients and other products, but that is only the beginning of the story. Because of the scale of ADM's operations, the Company is able to identify, isolate and extract highly valuable components that may exist in minute quantities within individual oilseeds.

ADM processes more than 90,000 tons of oilseeds each and every day of the year. Its extensive network of forty-six oilseed processing plants, strategically positioned throughout the primary agricultural regions of the world, allows ADM to efficiently match consumer demand for oil and oilseed products with supply, thereby ensuring efficient production for its customers.

The Company's oilseed processing operations yield several products, primarily vegetable oil, soy meal, edible soy protein and flour. As a first step in the process, oilseeds are crushed and refined, yielding cooking oil that can be packaged for home use or further processed into other products, such as cooking ingredients and packaged foods. Once the oil is removed from the seeds, the resulting high-protein meal is used in animal feeds and for pet foods.

From these basic bulk products, ADM produces several products and ingredients designed to unlock the maximum value contained in its raw material stream. Among these higher value offerings are emulsifiers like lecithin and monoglycerides, functional foods like soy protein isolates and d-alpha vitamin E and industrial products like biodiesel fuel and soy oil-based latex paints.

This method, using the co-product of an ADM product as the source for another, is central to the Company's approach of extracting the maximum value from the crops it processes. With its vertically integrated oilseed processing and transportation network, ADM is able to produce more products, at a higher quality and lower cost, than other agricultural processors.

Food Ingredients

BRINGING MORE TO THE TABLE

There is probably not one meal consumed in America that does not contain at least one ADM food ingredient. In fact, it's more likely that a meal would contain several ADM products. Archer Daniels Midland Company produces ingredients and products used by multinational consumer food and beverage manufacturers alike.

ADM's food ingredients are as basic as wheat flour and corn syrup; as complex as citric acid and the sugar-free sweetener sorbitol. ADM produces foods that are staples, as well as value-added ingredients that enhance and improve staple food.

The key strength of the ADM food ingredient line is its breadth. Because ADM is the world's premier food ingredient supplier, it is able to provide food manufacturers with a vast array of key ingredients, from citric acid to xanthan gum and everything in between.

Among the most widely used ADM food ingredients are wheat flour, corn flour and cornstarch, all used in a variety of baking applications. High fructose corn syrup (HFCS), a major ADM food product, is the predominant sweetener used in soft drinks. Citric acid and lactic acid (also made from corn) are used to adjust acid levels in both processed foods and beverages.

In addition to products made from oilseeds, corn and other grains, ADM is a major producer of foods made from other important commodities such as edible beans, sold either dry or canned; and rice, which is processed and shipped to markets around the globe.

Given ADM's role as a major processor of soybeans, it is fitting that its food ingredient line features several innovative soy-based products. In addition to a line of soy-based textured vegetable protein (TVP®) meat substitutes such as "veggie burger," ADM also produces its own line of soy-enriched pasta, marketed under the Soy7™ brand name.

Every year, ADM continues to add new food ingredients to its already extensive product catalog. At last count, ADM offered more than five hundred total food ingredients to food manufactures, with at least twenty new products planned for release every year.

1981
MENS MAJOR FAST PITCH
AMATEUR
SOFTBALL
ASSOCIATION

TEAM PLAYERS

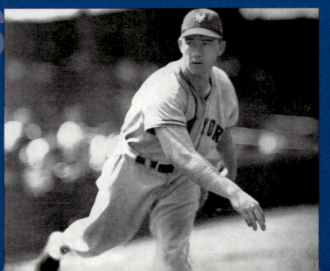

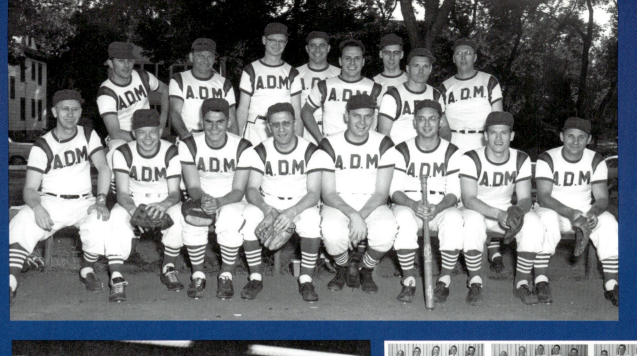

Ethanol, Biofuels and Industrials

FINDING HOME-GROWN SOLUTIONS

Although ADM's raw materials are agricultural products, their end use is not confined to the dinner table or the feedlot. The farmer's crops also offer a renewable alternative to the globe's dwindling supply of petroleum, both for use as a fuel and in an ever-growing number of industrial applications.

Ethanol is a perfect example of how ADM unlocks the potential of nature to provide renewable, sustainable solutions that improve the quality of life for all. A cleaner burning alternative to gasoline, ethanol currently is used as both an "oxygenate" and an octane booster for gasoline. Ethanol can extend gasoline supplies and reduce carbon monoxide emissions by as much as twenty-five percent. A growing number of oil refiners are using ethanol to replace Methyl Tertiary Butyl Ether (MTBE), a gasoline additive that has been shown to pollute groundwater. More than a dozen states have passed legislation to either ban or restrict the use of MTBE, accelerating this trend towards ethanol usage.

While ethanol is ADM's most recognized industrial product made from agricultural crops, it is far from the only one. Another example of renewable ADM-made fuels is the growing market for biodiesel.

Increasingly popular in certain areas of Europe and Asia, biodiesel is a vegetable oil-based fuel that can be substituted for the traditional petroleum-based product. Biodiesel burns much cleaner than regular diesel fuel and is not dependent on oil reserves. Interestingly enough, the original diesel engine developed in the 1890's used peanut oil as its fuel.

Many of ADM's food ingredients have industrial applications as well. Xanthan gum – often used to lend body and texture to salad dressings, dairy products and other processed foods – also serves as an industrial lubricant, a stabilizing agent for paint pigments and a viscosity modifier employed in oil productions. Lactic acid, used to raise the acidity of many foods, can also provide the key raw material in the production of plastics, solvents and other compounds typically made from petrochemicals.

The use of ADM products in industrial products is nearly limitless. These products are already found in the production of electronics, textiles, detergents, papers, metals and fire-fighting foams, to name just a few. ADM continues to work, in its research and development facilities and with its customers, to discover new industrial applications for its natural raw materials.

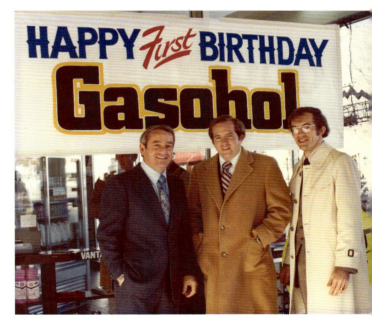

Martin Andreas, Edward Harjehausen and Doug Snyder celebrate Gasohol's first birthday at a Phillips' station in Cedar Rapids, Iowa.

Natural Health and Nutrition

GIVING BODIES WHAT'S GOOD FOR THEM

Nowhere is the potential of nature more fully evident than in the expanding area of ADM's nutrition products. An outgrowth of its oilseed crushing operations, which furnished an abundant source of raw materials, ADM's line of soy-based nutraceuticals can be readily incorporated into a wide variety of either food or supplement products. Most important of all, these nutraceuticals offer real health benefits to the consumer.

For example, vegetable oils are an excellent natural source of vitamin E, which is twice as potent in the human body as the more commonly used synthetic vitamin E. Additionally, vegetable oil is a source of phytosterols, a natural substance that helps promote normal levels of cholesterol in the bloodstream. Phytosterols are used in margarine-type spreads and dressings for salads, as well as additional products now being developed with new technologies.

Soy meal provides another source of functional food ingredients and products. ADM extracts isoflavones from soy meal; currently, more than 125 products are co-branded with ADM's Novasoy® isoflavone logo highlighted on the package. Isoflavones have been linked to such benefits as maintaining prostate health, cardiovascular health and bone density in post-menopausal women.

ADM also turns soy meal into soy isolates and concentrates, the basis for the ADM NutriSoy® brand of soy protein. ADM's own Soy7 pasta now features this brand name protein ingredient, with all products in the Soy7 pasta line containing at least seven grams of soy protein per serving. More and more third-party products already highlight NutriSoy soy protein content on the label, and several have found ways to leverage this content into usage of the FDA-approved soy protein heart-health claim. The many positive health benefits of soy are promoted extensively by ADM through its NutriSoy branding campaign, including its lead sponsorship of the American Heart Association's American Heart Walk program.

Beginning in 2002, a joint venture of ADM and Kao Corporation of Japan will begin producing Enova™ oil, a diacylglycerol (DAG) oil, for North America, Europe and other parts of the world. Enova oil has been shown to help promote beneficially low levels of body fat and triglycerides in the bloodstream. Derived from soy and canola oils, Enova oil can be used just like any other vegetable oil in a wide variety of applications, from baking to salad dressings and sauces. Already, this product has emerged as the best-selling premium oil in the Japanese market.

As science discovers and isolates additional health benefits found in natural products, ADM will continue to look for ways to provide these products to food manufacturers and consumers throughout the world.

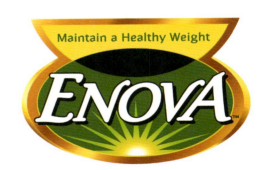

Feed Ingredients

DELIVERING ANSWERS TO THE FEEDLOT

Archer Daniels Midland Company is a major marketer of livestock feed ingredients. Its core businesses of corn processing, oilseed crushing, wheat milling and commodity merchandising provide the foundation for a dependable supply of these ingredients

ADM utilizes its global manufacturing, transportation and distribution network to efficiently deliver grain and oilseed meals to its customers. This network allows ADM to be a reliable and preferred supplier to the marketplace.

Using advanced fermentation technology, ADM converts dextrose derived from corn processing into the essential amino acids lysine and threonine. These amino acids are used by the swine and poultry industries to formulate diets that optimize performance while addressing environmental concerns.

ADM's family of feed ingredients also includes many co-products from the further processing or milling of corn and wheat. The nutritional value of these co-products provides the livestock producer with economical feed ingredient alternatives.

Grain

MANAGING THE HARVEST

Everything at Archer Daniels Midland Company begins with grain merchandising. One of the largest grain trading and origination organizations in the world, ADM's grain merchandising group is responsible for the purchase and delivery of the commodities that serve as ADM's raw materials. Through a global, interconnected network of ADM-owned facilities, joint ventures and partnerships, the grain merchandising group provides the link between the farmer and the ADM factory.

ADM owns and/or operates a network of more than five hundred grain elevators stretching across the United States, South America, Canada and other principal agricultural regions around the world. In addition, ADM operates export terminals that coordinate and handle the overseas shipment of oilseeds, grain and other commodities. This network enables ADM to trade grain on a global basis, shifting raw materials and production from market to market, optimizing the local supply and demand situation.

In addition to the vital role of grain merchandising in ADM's value-added business strategy, the group also plays a substantial role in the international system of grain and futures trading, helping to protect the Company from unforeseen changes in the global prices of grain and other commodities.

Cocoa

SHARING ONE OF NATURE'S PLEASURES

At Archer Daniels Midland Company, the mission to improve the quality of life extends far beyond the bare essentials of existence. Chocolate and cocoa, unlike the basic commodities processed by ADM, are foods associated with luxury and indulgence. However, the same expertise and scale that put ADM in a leadership position as a commodity processor have been successfully transferred to the cocoa industry, resulting in increased productivity and profitability.

The fact that many of ADM's customers worldwide were already buyers of other ADM products such as corn sweeteners and emulsifiers has been a real positive as ADM has expanded into the cocoa industry. Through acquisition and expansion, ADM is now the world's largest non-retail processor of cocoa beans. ADM Cocoa's size and scope puts the Company in a unique position to provide its customers with a secure, full spectrum of products and services that include ingredients, processing applications and expertise in developing new products.

In addition to processing cocoa beans into cocoa powder, cocoa butter and cocoa liquor for sale to chocolate manufacturers, ADM also offers a comprehensive range of chocolate and cocoa ingredients to the confectionery, bakery, dairy and beverage industries. ADM Cocoa's operations provide secure sourcing, efficient processing, technical support and timely deliveries to meet its customers' current and future requirements. Its ability to offer specific solutions to customer applications is unmatched in the industry.

ADM Cocoa is truly a global organization, with facilities in five continents serving seventy countries. ADM Cocoa products are marketed under the brands Ambrosia®, De Zaan® and Merckens®. Its global network of cocoa facilities enables the Company to develop and produce chocolate and cocoa products specifically tailored to meet the customer's requests, including the ability to meet regional preferences in taste, texture and appearance. ADM Cocoa's skilled technical staff and knowledgeable sales force work with customers, ensuring they receive the right product for the right application.

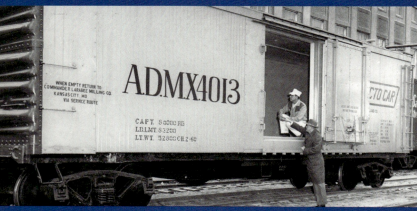

A.D.M.X 4013

In 1974, the original three ARTCO boats were named after the wives of ADM employees: Inez Andreas, wife of Dwayne Andreas; Ginny Stone, wife of Neville Stone, who was the first president of ARTCO and Sally Archer, Bud Archer's wife. These lower river towboats are still in operation today. The boats are armed with 8400 horsepower, pushing as many as 42 loaded barges on the Lower Mississippi River between St. Louis and New Orleans.

Transportation

Bringing the Bounty Home

The ADM transportation network gives the Company the power to efficiently deliver agricultural products on a global scale.

As one of the most vertically integrated agricultural processors on the globe, ADM is capable of transporting crops from the farmer's field, processing them into a variety of value-added products and delivering them to customers worldwide.

In order to achieve this, ADM has developed the world's largest agricultural transportation system, using a combination of over-the-road trucks, railcars, river barges and ocean-going vessels to transport millions of tons of grain and value-added products each year.

ADM and its subsidiaries own and operate approximately 2,180 barges, 650 tractor-trailers, 17,000 railcars and 85 tow boats. In addition to this Company-owned fleet, ADM shipments also occupy a total of five million trucks, 500,000 railcars and 12,000 barges a year. Its export and distribution centers in North America, South America, Europe and the Far East enable the ADM network to supply all the world's major markets.

Our Commitment to the Future

MOVING FORWARD IS OUR NATURE

While nature holds answers, they often aren't apparent to the casual observer. That is why Archer Daniels Midland Company has made a significant commitment to research and development. Using state-of-the art equipment, ADM scientists and researchers conduct pioneering work on the commodities they process, developing new production techniques and innovative products. As a result of this effort, ADM has applied for more patents in the last four years alone than it had received in the entire prior history of the Company.

ADM is supplementing this internal research effort through strategic partnerships with other companies and organizations that share its goals. In many cases, these partnerships pair exciting new technologies developed outside ADM with ADM's proven strengths in raw material supply, processing and distribution.

ADM's commitment to cost-effective food production has also led the Company to search for innovative agricultural processing techniques to support increasing population and economic growth. Toward that goal, two projects are now in operation at ADM's headquarters in Decatur, Illinois – each one demonstrating ADM's dedication to build the lowest-cost, most efficient structural model in the world of agricultural processing.

At the ADM hydrofarm, a ten-acre indoor facility produces thousands of heads of lettuce, cucumbers and herbs in a hydroponic environment. Using waste heat and carbon dioxide from the nearby corn processing plant, ADM creates a carefully controlled environment ideal for the growth of vegetable crops. The same facility also is home to an aquaculture center where Tilapia, a mild-flavored whitefish, is produced for sale to grocers and seafood wholesalers.

ADM also operates an innovative co-generation power plant that allows the Company to heat and power its largest processing facility using a mixture of limestone, high-sulfur coal and discarded automobile tires. This fuel actually burns 3.5 times cleaner than a typical coal-fired power plant, while lowering ADM's overall energy costs and lessening its vulnerability to the market-price fluctuations of traditional fuels.

In these and other ways, Archer Daniels Midland Company is demonstrating that the earth's bounty can provide viable solutions to man-made problems. Nature has answers. Is anyone listening? Yes: ADM.

FACILITIES AND INFRASTRUCTURE

Archer Daniels Midland Company owns, operates or leases more than 500 grain elevators and 268 processing plants worldwide. In addition, ADM maintains sales and marketing offices in twenty countries and in every continent except Antarctica, with wholly owned or joint-venture interests in seventy-one countries.

With over 24,000 employees spread across this worldwide infrastructure, ADM is poised to offer localized customized products and services to customers on a truly global basis. As one of the most vertically integrated agricultural processors on the planet, ADM delivers an overall advantage in product diversity, quality and pricing that no other processor can match. And with the continued dedication of these unparalleled resources to its collective mission, ADM will continue to provide nature-based solutions for the benefit of all.

service above and beyond..

Right there where the Commander is pointing . . . and right now . . . we're adding a gigantic wheat storage unit to our mills and daylight packing plant at Kansas City, to *double* present storage capacity.

This doubles our assurance, too, that we will be able to provide you with the same dependable, high quality flours in January that you're accustomed to get from us in June— or in any other month, for that matter.

ADM LOGO

i'm trying to...ex

BEFORE 1962

1962 – 2001

THE NATURE OF WHAT'S TO COME™

EVOLUTION OF THE ADM LOGO

The first logo used for Archer Daniels Midland Company was the archer figure. The logo featured a yeoman with a feathered cap, skin tights and a longbow. Interestingly enough, ADM could not use the yeoman in conjunction with its food products since International Milling Company, another firm based in Minneapolis, Minnesota, had a similar figure that it used to advertise its "Robin Hood" flour.

The archer logo was changed on March 1, 1962, since the figure did not contribute to a cohesive identity of ADM's line of business. The new logo featured a highly stylized diamond-shaped blue leaf containing four black circles connected by black lines – a design meant to represent chemical molecules coming from a natural resource.

In April of 2001, ADM announced a new corporate logo, tagline and advertising campaign designed to underscore the Company's deep commitment to nature and global agriculture. The new corporate identity also signals ADM's increased emphasis on innovation and product development. The new logo incorporates elements of the old, including ADM's signature blue diamond, while adding an easily recognizable green leaf to reflect the Company's agricultural roots.

2001 – PRESENT

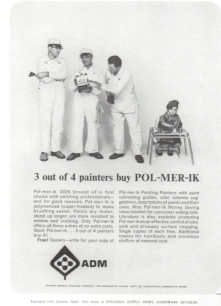

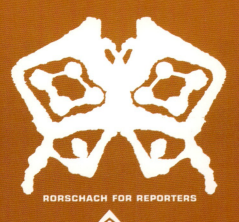

RORSCHACH FOR REPORTERS

ADM

ADM Advertising

The Company's advertising has changed significantly over the years. For the first eighty years, ADM had no corporate-wide campaign or theme. Instead, individual divisions would produce ads for their target industry. Among the more prominent and memorable ads from this era were those in support of its Commander Larabee brand of flour. The ads, featuring a cartoon illustration of a helpful "Commander," highlighted the performance benefits of the flour. Another memorable campaign from the flour division included the series of ads featuring real-life silent-film comedian Buster Keaton. In the ads, Mr. Keaton's dour visage clearly communicated the disadvantages of bread made without ADM flour.

In the 1980s, ADM introduced its first corporate-wide campaign: the famous "Supermarket to the World." One of the longest-running and most memorable advertising campaigns in history, the campaign became a fixture on Sunday morning television, PBS news broadcasts and National Public Radio. As examples on this page illustrate, the campaign was also successfully translated to print magazines.

Replacing the "Supermarket to the World" was no easy task, but in 2001 the Company unveiled its new campaign and theme: "The Nature of What's to Come." Featuring cutting-edge animation techniques and thought-provoking topics, this campaign clearly reflects the Company's commitment to developing natural-based solutions to many of the world's pressing problems, including hunger, malnutrition and the environment.

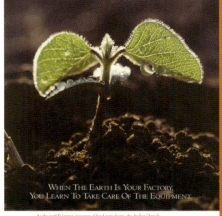

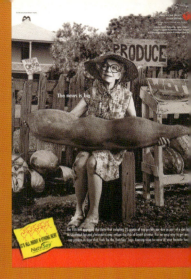

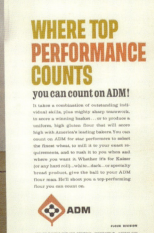
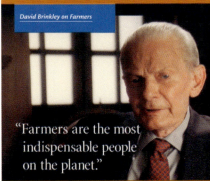
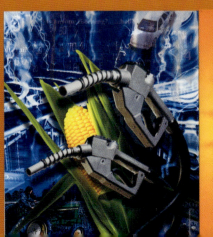

ADM and Buster Keaton

In 1964, the ADM Flour Division featured an 18-month advertising campaign featuring the unsmiling and expressive face of veteran showman, Buster Keaton. The story began when Mr. Keaton was scheduled to appear at the Minnesota State Fair in late August of 1963. ADM quickly approached him with an offer to do a series of advertisements and to their delight, Mr. Keaton accepted. John Rushinko, product advertising supervisor with ADM's Advertising Department, noted, "Mr. Keaton kept us in stitches. He was a real card when operating and a remarkable model. He sensed each situation quickly and easily switched from one pose to another. He always wears his pancake straw hat and will be photographed in no other. He never smiles in pictures, but off camera, he's a jovial individual, and despite beliefs to the contrary, he can smile and often does."

The series of advertisements were viewed as ground breaking at the time and after the series ran, other companies attempted to emulate.

CORPORATE COMMITMENT

GIVING IS IN OUR NATURE

This century of innovation has also been a century of giving. As one of the world's premier agribusinesses, ADM is dedicated to improving the lives of others, not only through agricultural advances but also through humanitarian efforts.

During the twenty-first century, as the world faces ever-increasing changes and challenges, ADM's long-standing traditions of corporate giving and employee volunteerism, both domestically and internationally, take on even greater significance as humankind works to build strong societies and healthy communities.

In 2002, the year of ADM's one hundred-year anniversary, ADM employees and retirees around the world again have demonstrated their commitment to volunteerism and giving. In fact, many employees have served as volunteers, giving literally hundreds of thousands of dollars and their time and considerable talents to their communities. This is a source of tremendous pride for everyone at ADM.

As might be expected, ADM has been a longtime supporter of government-sponsored food relief programs, including Public Law 480. This program seeks to expand foreign markets for U.S. agricultural prod-

ucts and to fight hunger, as well as encourage the economic advancement of developing nations. ADM's support goes far beyond government-sponsored programs. Recently, ADM helped the people of Somalia fend off starvation during their epic crisis.

ADM has contributed millions of dollars in both food and charitable donations to such organizations as the American Red Cross, the CARE Foundation, the Corporation to End World Hunger and Mother Teresa Missionaries of Charity. These donations have helped hungry people throughout El Salvador, Haiti, Guatemala, the Dominican Republic, Nicaragua and Cambodia.

In other examples of ADM's largess, ADM donated one hundred metric tons of powdered soy beverages for distribution to children in Cuba, one of the largest single food donations ever made by an American company. The Company has also made significant contributions to the American Soybean Association's World Initiative for Soy in Human Health projects in Africa, shipping several containers of soy flour, soybean oil and textured soybean protein to Zimbabwe, Mozambique and Botswana. ADM also made a three million-dollar commitment of food and money to the

World Food Program earmarked for Angola, one of the most devastated areas in recent history.

Additionally, ADM and NutriSoy® soy protein have become a national sponsor of the American Heart Association's American Heart Walk. Besides partnering with the American Heart Association to fight cardiovascular disease, ADM is helping to generate consumer awareness of heart-healthy products.

Locally, ADM and its employees have contributed and continue to contribute to hundreds of area organizations annually, including local food banks in and around the Company headquarters, America's Harvest, The Boys & Girls Clubs of America, Special Olympics of Central Illinois, Decatur Area Arts Council, Decatur Area Crimestoppers, Decatur-Macon County Senior Center, YMCA, Millikin University and the United Way, where ADM is a Pace Setter.

Pace Setter. There couldn't be a better descriptor of ADM. The Company can be counted on to be involved in important global issues that impact its business by promoting the world's health and prosperity. ADM welcomed the imminent entry of China

into the World Trade Organization and permitting the Cuban people to have access to food supplies. ADM encouraged the development of a healthy investment climate in Russia. The success of agriculture depends on trade, and each of these efforts to promote cooperation among the world's nations will improve life on our planet.

As ADM leads the way through the twenty-first century, the Company remains true to its mission: "To unlock the potential of nature to improve the quality of life." As a responsible corporate citizen, the world can look for more of the same from ADM. Truly, it is "The Nature of What's to Come."

Will you help
a damsel in distress?

This is a delicate matter ...but we know you'll understand.

Here at ADM, we spend several hundred thousand dollars a year for telephone

calls and telegrams. And we wish we could get **MORE** 's and 's...

but we **CAN'T** Frankly, our switchboards are overloaded...and our operators are

swamped. So-oo-o, may we ask a favor? If, for the present, you limit

all necessary family calls to brief messages on urgent matters only, we shall be

VERY VERY VERY grateful!

ARCHER-DANIELS-MIDLAND CO.

archer cover girl contestants

ARCHER presents the candidates YOU submitted for our June cover girl. Now . . . you vote! Select your favorite by number (number of each girl appears ABOVE her picture in each case). Put this number on the enclosed postcard and mail back to ARCHER immediately! Winner of the most votes will be June cover girl. She'll also receive a $50 first prize. Second and third place winners will receive $25 and $10 respectively.

So here are ADM's cover girl candidates. There are no doubt many many more that were submitted but ARCHER hopes you'll find your choice among these. Write the number of your favorite and mail that card today! And—save this ARCHER, because we'll be identifying the girls according to the numbers of their photos in next month's issue.

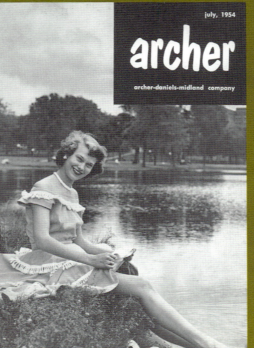

july, 1954

archer

archer-daniels-midland company

87

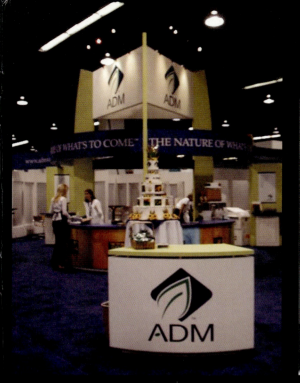

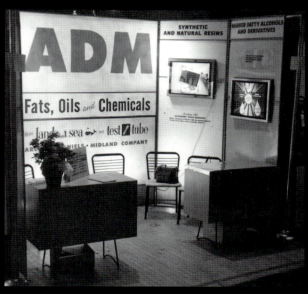

Acknowledgements

ADM would like to thank the Decatur Herald & Review newspaper, Martin L. Andreas, John H. Daniels, E. M. Drescher, Ginger Gisinger, Harry Ground, Burnell Kraft, Dick Newman, James R. Randall, Robert Sailing, the family of Doc Schopmeyer, the Revoir Historical Collection and all of the countless employees and retirees who contributed archival items and photographs.

November 7, 2002

Bibliography

Books

Kahn, Jr., E.J. *Supermarketer to the World*, Warner Books, 1991.

Other Organizations, Web Sites and Documents

Advertising supplement, *Decatur Herald & Review*, March 1999

From Land, Sea, and Test Tube : The Story of Archer Daniels Midland Company, Archer Daniels Midland Company, 1957

U.S. Library of Congress, http://www.loc.gov

U.S. Department of Agriculture, http://www.usda.gov

Economic Research Service, http://www.ers.usda.gov

National Park Service, http://www.nps.gov

Food and Agricultural Organization of the United Nations, http://www.fao.org

Institute for Agriculture and Trade Policy, http://www.iatp.org

Corporate Agribusiness Research Project, http://www.ea1.com/CARP/index.html

American Farm Bureau, http://www.fb.com